You Can Take It With You

YOU CAN TAKE IT WITH YOU
By
Timothy Green Beckley, Maria D'Andrea, Sir L. J. Baldry

Copyright 2017 by Timothy Green Beckley
dba Global Communications/Conspiracy Journal

All rights reserved. No part of these manuscripts may be copied or reproduced by any mechanical or digital methods and no exerpts or quotes may be used in any other book or manuscript without permission in writing by the Publisher, Global Communications/Conspiracy Journal, except by a reviewer who may quote brief passages in a review.

Published in the United States of America By
Global Communications/Conspiracy Journal
Box 753 · New Brunswick, NJ 08903

Staff Members
Timothy G. Beckley, Publisher
Carol Ann Rodriguez, Assistant to the Publisher
Sean Casteel, General Associate Editor
Tim R. Swartz, Graphics and Editorial Consultant
William Kern, Editorial and Art Consultant

Sign Up On The Web For Our Free Weekly Newsletter
and Mail Order Version of Conspiracy Journal
and Bizarre Bazaar
www.ConspiracyJournal.com

**Subscribe To Our YouTube Channel
Mr UFOs Secret Files**

Order Hot Line: 1-732-602-3407
PayPal: MrUFO8@hotmail.com

CONTENTS

Prelude— 1

Enter The Wealthiest Man In God's Kingdom
Timothy Green Beckley 7

There's No Way I Was Born Just To Pay My Bills And Die
Maria D'Andrea 39

Finding Heaven's Pot Of Gold
Sir L. J. Baldry 65

YOU CAN TAKE IT WITH YOU

"In my house there are many mansions," saith the Lord in the complex maze of dimensions that populate the Heavens.

The Summerland can be almost anything and anywhere you can imagine it to be.

After death it is a matter of finding the right doorway to your final resting place.

Early on the Spiritualist movement in America described the afterlife as a beautiful world that they called the Summerland.

THE SUMMER LAND ZONE WITHIN THE MILKY WAY.

YOU CAN TAKE IT WITH YOU

TURN THOSE "PENNIES FROM HEAVEN" INTO A CONSTANT CASH FLOW YOU CAN TAKE IT WITH YOU WHEN YOU GO, GO, GO
By Timothy Green Beckley

"As he thinketh in his heart, so is he."
Proverbs 23:7

They say the rich get richer, and the poor get poorer, but that death is the great equalizer because you can't take it with you when you go, go, go.

But even the most holier-than-thou might have to rethink this idiom upon reaching the end of life's pages, just as you will upon reaching the end of this book. For it is a generally concealed secret that you can take it with you over to the other side if you live "properly" before closing death's door behind you.

Truth is, the end of the rainbow doesn't

YOU CAN TAKE IT WITH YOU

have to be at the foot of your final resting place; it can just as easily shine through to that place we most commonly refer to as Heaven, though that interpolation is open for grabs.

Every religion has a different concept of life after life. Many fine folks who are Christians seem to think that when we die we float off onto a cloud and sit around listening to ethereal music, reuniting with loved ones only to wait for the day of judgment. Their reality is very sterile. There is no sex. No drinking or eating. No paying rent (thank God!), because there is no money "up there," so—finally!—we can all be equal. Naturally the rich don't much like this theory (can't blame them one bit), and the formerly poor are still jealous that they never became a "big shot" anywhere.

The idea seems to be we are all on an equal plane. It won't make any difference if you were a Mitt Romney one-percenter or hung out on the unemployment line. Its all the same on Millionaire's Row.

I for one crave a little bit of that pie in the sky in the great by and by. And if I've lived a good and exemplary life and didn't break any of the ten commandments (can we cut them back to maybe six or seven for those "sinners" amongst us?), not only do I deserve a seat in the orchestra instead of the balcony, but I should

YOU CAN TAKE IT WITH YOU

still be able to sip a glass of wine made from the ripest of grapes in Heaven's vineyard.

I also should still be able to "pay my way" wherever my spirit wishes to roam in the afterlife. And here's the rub—you don't have to keep your money in a vault, or haul it around in a suitcase, for money "upstairs" is more in the category of bitcoins than physical cash. After all, gold or silver is too bulky, if it fell out of your hands it would crash through the clouds and probably hit someone on the head (oh excuse me, sounds like Charles Fort writing on mysterious falls from the sky).

Now here is what spiritually minded individuals consider Heaven to be all about.

Heaven in the psychic world or spiritualist community is known as the Summerland. Its sort of a multi-tiered place where souls venture once they have aborted their bodies. Its more or less like taking a vacation cruise, and on this cruise liner there are many different "floors" or levels. You can "rent" a single occupancy or if you set your mind to it you can take the elevator to the Summerland's penthouse.

For the most part it's determined by how you behaved in your earthly existence. How good you were to others. How charitable you were. Whether you put your money to good use or not. For example, if you were a rich man and

YOU CAN TAKE IT WITH YOU

hoarded all those green backs then you don't get the same rewards as someone who went out and toiled the field with the poor and down trodden or helped the sick or the orphans.

If all "goes well," you can take it with you in the respect that the more you accomplished on the physical, the higher you will rebound in the afterlife, ultimately to have all that you have always desired—and without the discomfort and pain, and surrounded by all that is beautiful and the ones you love the most.

Everyone will look like the time in their lives that they felt the best about themselves. In his major work, **"The Great Harmonia,"** Emanuel Swedenborg (1688-1910) determines that the Summerland is the pinnacle of human spiritual achievement in the afterlife. That is, it is the highest level or "sphere" of the afterlife we can hope to enter.

One of the founding fathers of the spiritualist movement, Andrew Jackson Davis put his stamp of approval on the existence of the Summerland when he described his vision of it thusly: *'The Summer Land, more especially those portions of it which are in connection with the inhabitants of earth, appears to my interior eyes like a neighboring planet. It is the next room in the house not made with our hands. But there are an infinite number of other rooms.*

YOU CAN TAKE IT WITH YOU

'Characteristics and peculiarities of the lower territories or sections may not prevail in any of the higher divisions of the sphere. When the eyes of the seer look higher, forthwith many of those things which so distinctly prevailed, as peculiarly adapted to the neighboring existence, utterly cease to exist.

'In that section of the other sphere which lies next to us, the law of social attraction is as powerfully operative as it is in this world. It is not easy to tell why, but the dwellers are gregarious. They are attracted socially to remain very near each other. But higher up, rather, away in more refined sections, they are influenced by other, more lofty, interests.'

In the Summerland it is said you will hook up with those spirits you desire to be surrounded by the most as part of a reeducation program. If you are into Jesus he will be there. Buddha, even Ronald Reagan or Mahatma Gandhi can come strolling by in the green, green rolling fields of your new home in what is most easily defined as Heaven.

So, as you see, your riches are manifold. That which you have made for yourself on the terrestrial planet will to some extent determine your perception of what the life everlasting will be able to offer you.

YOU CAN TAKE IT WITH YOU

ENTER THE "WEALTHIEST" MAN IN GOD'S KINGDOM

It's a balmy Sunday afternoon in New York City. You're walking around the corner of 175th Street and Broadway in Washington Heights. Suddenly, a car pulls up to the curb. It's a sleek, chauffeur driven Rolls Royce. The figure of a tall, quite handsome black man emerges from the back seat. He is dressed in a flashy pink, custom-tailored, fashionable suit. It must have cost him a small fortune. You recognize him immediately.

Within seconds you realize that you're not dealing with some poor people's messiah.

For, clinging to several fingers on both hands you notice huge diamond rings—the kind of jewelry that seems to wink back at you with a life of its own. Indeed, whoever was responsible for coining the cliche, *'You can't buy your way into Heaven,'* quite obviously had never heard of Frederick Eikerenkotter better known to his countless legions of devoted followers simply as Reverend Ike.

Not since the heyday of Father Divine has a black evangelist created such a fuss and stir. Extreme and flamboyant, with a remarkable vocabulary, a moving, forceful voice and the gift of dynamic eloquence, he is the subject of hot and lively press coverage wherever he goes.

And while all of this coverage hasn't been especially positive—Harlem's *Amsterdam News*, for example, has run several stories bit-

YOU CAN TAKE IT WITH YOU

terly attacking his outrageous style—there has been enough attention generated to make Reverend Ike a pseudo-celebrity among blacks and whites alike.

There is absolutely no getting around the indisputable fact that he makes for an impulsive personality, adorned in clothes he himself admits to shelling out $1,000 a week for.

Having left this realm behind on July 28, 2009, unlike his professional image in later years, Ike's background is unimpressive, to say the least. Born in Ridgeland, South Carolina in 1935 (to a Baptist preacher of Dutch Indian-Afro ancestry), Ike was only five when his father walked out on an unsuccessful marriage. For a long time thereafter Ike's mother managed to support the family by teaching school. Her earnings: a paltry sum of $65 per month.

When I met and spent some time with the "rags to riches" Reverend, he was pretty much at the pinnacle of his ministerial career which included all sorts of advertising and self promotions. And while the media could be harsh on his pitch, his followers tossed money into the collection bucket as if there was no tomorrow. I know because I passed it on a few times during his services and it was over flowing – and we're not talking about change or loose singles.

The Reverend wasn't going to miss a

YOU CAN TAKE IT WITH YOU

golden opportunity to collect his tithings for the day and he had no misgivings about NOT taking his "glorious wealth" with him.

Never one to take on a defeatist attitude, the dynamic evangelist remembers dreaming of some day driving "one of them big cars" which would constantly race by.

Even when Mother Eikerenkotter and little Fred were mud-splashed, as the autos heartlessly rumbled down the narrow roadways of his home town, a negative attitude about life, and the cruelty man is capable of, never took hold of him.

There was high school, a New York seminary which Ike attended for four years, and a hitch in the Air Force as a chaplain's assistant. Honorably discharged, and with $200 he managed to seal his path, as though guided by unseen hands which led him to Savannah, Georgia. There he purchased radio time and became

YOU CAN TAKE IT WITH YOU

an instant broadcasting success as a faith healer over the airwaves.

Slowly, tirelessly, and with self-assurance, he expanded his radio coverage until he was heard on more than a dozen radio stations throughout the South. In 1962, Ike founded the United church of Jesus Christ for All People, in South Carolina. Two years later, he moved on to Boston and organized the Miracle Temple. Finally, in 1966, he launched the United church Science of Living Institute in New York City, which he eventually headquartered in the old Loew's Palace Theater which he purchased in 1969.

Reverend Ike miraculously converted the former 5,500 seat theater into a virtual palace. It took time, money and effort, but it was done. The decor is Louis XV with more than two million dollars in gold-plated trim.

In keeping with what the American public had come to expect, Reverend Ike did not go about preaching his sermons in the conventional manner. For example, instead of singing typical "Praise The Lord" hymns, Ike's choir is more than likely to belt forth a jazzed-up rendition of *"Pennies from Heaven."* Says Reverend Ike, 'Nothing inspires me more than money!" What's more, he went out of his way to pass this feeling on to those in his then rapidly increas-

YOU CAN TAKE IT WITH YOU

ing congregation.

Upon meeting, Ike was quick to point out that to his way of thinking there was nothing wrong with aspiring to be rich. "Personally, I think the lack of money is the root of all evil."

In effect, if you can't help yourself you're never going to be able to help others.

And while refusing to reveal either his personal worth, or the church's, there can be little doubt but that Ike's revenue at his peak totaled into the millions yearly. Broadcast daily over 1700 radio stations, his "love of money" messages traveled across the radio air waves, reaching homes in every state, as well as Canada, and even occasionally European cities. His TV specials were so popular that the Neilson ratings show they often outdrew the most popular network programs.

Some have called him "phony," out to exploit the public, while others looked to him with great respect and reverence. Often referred to as "the black man's Norman Vincent Peale," Reverend Ike is, in person, charming and cordial. He is also a great wit. As this interview indicates, Reverend Ike went out of his way to be open and frank, never once trying to avoid my line of questioning.

Beckley: "Why do you feel the need to

YOU CAN TAKE IT WITH YOU

dress so flamboyantly, to drive a Rolls Royce and live in such a lavish style? Some folks might say that you live handsomely while others live in ghettos and barely have enough to eat. Isn't your life style in contradiction with the way most other ministers would do things?"

Rev. Ike: "It's not a contradiction to the way I would do things. I do what I do because I love it, and I believe it's right. There's an interesting incident I'll never forget. I was sitting in the back of the church's limousine downtown and a strange black kid came over to me and said, 'Are you Reverend Ike?' I told him I was. 'Well then,' he commented, 'do you think it's right for you to be riding around in a car like this?'

"I questioned him as to why he would ask such a thing, to which he replied, 'Well, aren't you supposed to help the poor?' I thought about that for a moment and then said, "Would it help the poor more if I got out of the Rolls Royce and got on a bicycle?"

Beckley: "Have you ever known what it's like to be impoverished?"

Rev Ike: "Certainly. I grew up with poverty all around me. I attended school in South Carolina, where lunch was only seven cents. But I couldn't' even afford that. I often went hungry. I couldn't think of very much else when my stomach was grumbling. So, yes, I've experienced material poverty, but I've come to believe people can love the Lord a lot better when they have the money to pay their bills and meet their needs.

"Luckily, I held the thought that no matter how bad my situation was, it could get better. I remember the times my mother would walk me four miles to school each day, and the people passed by in their fine cars and splashed water on us from the muddy road. Even then, I tried not to identify with the one who had the water splashed on him. I identified with those rich folks riding in the cars.

"Later, while going to Bible school in New York, I would stand outside the plush Plaza Hotel and imagine how it would feel to be inside eating. I knew better than to think of myself simply as the hungry little black boy with his nose pressed up against the plate glass window looking in. I didn't have subway fare, but I knew in my heart the days would get better. They did!"

Beckley: "Your approach to Evangelism is rather unique—perhaps strange to some people. Fundamentalists and other clergymen might accuse you of heresy. Just how literally do you take the Bible?"

Rev Ike: "To my way of thinking, the Bible is a book of psychology. So I take the Bible as

YOU CAN TAKE IT WITH YOU

more psychological than theological. The characters and events in the Bible represent various movements in the psychology of man. For example. I believe in Jesus very much, but I take it a step further than the so-called fundamental Christians. I believe that, in reality, every man is what Jesus was. To me, Jesus represents the divinity of man—every man—and not just one individual who lived two thousand years ago."

Beckley: "That's an interesting point you make about the message of the Bible being psychological. Can you cite chapter and verse as an example of your positive approach to living?"

Rev Ike: "Well, how about Psalms 92:12? *'The righteous shall flourish like the palm tree, he shall grow like a cedar in Lebanon.'* I like the word "flourish." Nowhere in the Bible does it tell us we must be poor. In fact, it doesn't even say that we are expected to get by just by the skin of our teeth. Do you remember back when we were growing up, they told us that the Scripture said that even the righteous will scarcely make it into heaven?

"Now that's the kind of religion I'm against. That's the kind of religion you have to get rid of. The Scripture doesn't say any such thing about the people of God just barely getting by. Success and prosperity are within you

YOU CAN TAKE IT WITH YOU

and all around you at all times. You have to learn to focus your mental attention on the positive, Once you do your life will be better for it.

"Scripture says, *'The righteous shall flourish.'* Even if you think you have good Bible religion, you don't have it until you start flourishing. I don't know where folks get this "poverty religion." They come to New York to get the welfare religion and cling to the welfare like the old rugged cross. The Bible says the righteous—those who work with the positive right ideas in their minds—shall flourish. It means that

YOU CAN TAKE IT WITH YOU

you can have plenty, if you just think with a clear, open consciousness. It's a matter of self-awareness.

"And I say, success and prosperity are within you and all around you at all times, in spite of the pessimistic things that we must contend with. And once you learn to focus your mental attention on success, you'll begin seeing it, and you will increase your own experience of it. Some of the wealthiest people in the world today started out as poor as dirt.

"But too many times when people see the so-called rich, they don't think about that.. They forget. They just curse the rich. And I tell them, as long as you curse the rich and criticize the rich, you'll never be one of them."

Beckley: "Wouldn't you say then that the acceptance of so-called orthodox religion has been a hindrance—at least to an extent—to the material development of the Afro American population?"

Rev Ike: "Yes. But not just to blacks. I believe in green power, not black power.

"I don't think that the needs of the blacks are any different than the needs of Indians, Orientals, Puerto Ricans or whites. Everybody has the same basic needs: health, happiness, love, success and on the material level, money. Unfortunately, in many cases, our religion has taught us to draw back from our natural divinity. Some of us have been taught to think, *'I'm not good enough. Lord, I'm not worthy.'* Well, baby, let me tell you, you get only what you believe you deserve.

"If you don't believe you deserve a thing, you might as well stop praying for it. That's why psychiatrists tell us it's not good to have an inferiority complex. Yet, our religions gave us such a complex. If you don't watch out, religion will make you think you're supposed to crawl around, praying and begging some God in the sky, all the time offering, *'Now, Lord, I know I'm not worthy.'* In my services I cast away all doubt. I preach positive awareness, that's what I preach.

"When a person starts to see himself in a positive light, then he can become independent.

"If you give a man a fish, you feed him for a day. Teach him how to fish, and you feed him for life. That's one of my favorite sayings. In my church we don't believe in soup or breadlines. Nor do we attempt to get folks on welfare. I want people to believe in themselves, not the next guy. When you've had a dose of Rev. Ike's teaching, you know it. Like I tell people. 'You can't lose with the stuff I use!' "

YOU CAN TAKE IT WITH YOU

Beckley: "Keeping in mind your philosophy, what do you have to say about the existence of God and Heaven and Hell?"

Rev. Ike: "Its a matter of interpretation. I find it hard to believe that there is an old man sitting on a chair up in the sky. I tell people that God is within you. As for Heaven and Hell, no one has preached more hellfire and brimstone and damnation than I have. While I was preaching and telling people that they were going to hell, I would look around and I saw that people were already in hell. I saw that people were in one hell of a fix. People were sick and suffering, depressed, suppressed, repressed and regressed.

YOU CAN TAKE IT WITH YOU

"I said, 'There is no use preaching to these people and telling them they are going to hell They are already there. I need to get something to help them out of that hell of a condition.' That's why I give out the message that, 'The righteous shall flourish. He shall grow as a cedar in Lebanon.' I remember I was never more impressed than when I heard a very wonderful minister say, 'When a person gets tired of hell, he'll look for heaven.' Well, I've found my heaven. NOW. Don't wait for pie in the sky when you die. I tell 'em, 'Get yours now, with plenty of ice cream on top!' "

Beckley: "In addition to the Sunday services held at your United church in Washington Heights, you also preside over what you call Money Conditioning Services. What exactly are these?"

Rev Ike: "These gatherings are very academic. The theme is money, and the services are held to condition people's minds so that they're receptive to money. If it's possible to air-condition a building, I think it's possible to money-condition the mind."

Beckley: "How do you go about doing this, especially if a person has not heard of your philosophy of self-awareness before, and has become conditioned to living in the lpit of poverty?"

YOU CAN TAKE IT WITH YOU

Rev Ike: "I teach people that they have a multi-million-dollar talent. I get them to repeat after me. Words have very special meanings.

*(Editor's Note: Read Maria D' Andrea's **"Supernatural Words Of Power"** for a detailed explanation of this philosophy).*

"We visualize and speak only of riches. Remember, in the gospel, Jesus made the statement: *'He shall have whatsoever he sayeth.'* If you say something. and believe it strongly enough, you will get it. If you keep insisting. 'I'm poor,' then that's what you are. I've had people come up to me and say, 'Rev. Ike, I just can't hold onto money ... money slips away from me.'

"People are so used to reacting negatively that it requires hard work to get them to alter their thinking process. That's what I try to do. There's only one mouth that can curse you, and that's your own big mouth. As the Bible says. 'Thou art ensnared by the words of thy mouth.'

"If you can use your mouth to impoverish yourself, you can use that same mouth to enrich yourself."

(Publishers Note: *This philosophy—as this book illustrates—can be adapted to your final trip "abroad" from which you will not likely return, minus the possibility of a NDE, Near Death Experience).*

YOU CAN TAKE IT WITH YOU

Beckley: "Can you tell us of any cases where people used your self-awareness philosophy and actually prospered?"

Rev Ike: "The files of the church are full of them. We have so, so, many success stories that it's hard for people to accept them at first, but we always make our records open to reporters like yourself. I remember ten years ago in Boston, while I was still having prayer lines to pray for people (of course, that would be impossible now with the thousands that come to these services) this particular lady came up in the prayer line for me to pray for her. She was the funniest and raggediest looking little thing I guess I had ever seen. She was so raggedy that when she lifted her hands to praise the Lord and to pray, her blouse was air conditioned.

YOU CAN TAKE IT WITH YOU

"Well, she asked me to pray for her, saying, 'Rev. lke, some money is due me and I desperately need it. I'm out of work and my landlord is going to throw me on the street. I want you to pray that I get the money that's due to me.' I said, 'Honey, you sure need it!'

"She really looked like a ragamuffin to me. So I prayed a real good prayer. The very next night I had another meeting and as I sat in my chair and looked around. I saw a lady in the front row waving to me. This woman was dressed to kill. Mink was crawling all over her. She was waving and calling, 'Rev. Ike, Rev. Ike!' I took another look and thought. 'Now, what does this woman mean by getting fresh with me right here in church?' She just wouldn't quit waving and shouting.

"Finally I listened harder and could make out what she was saying. She was shouting, 'Rev. Ike, I got it. I got it! I got it. I got it! I got my money! I got it all today!'

"So I looked at her a little closer I and discovered that here was the same woman that had come to me for prayer just the night before, just as raggedy as could be. Now, she was as beautiful as could be. She couldn't hold back her joy. She dashed up to the pulpit and handed me an envelope stuffed full of money. I took a good look and nearly fainted at what I saw. In those

YOU CAN TAKE IT WITH YOU

days, people didn't give much money. But here was a fist full.

"Later, this woman told me, 'Rev. Ike, you prayed for me last night. and I got my money today!' And she looked like it. She was all dressed to kill. Everything that was due her. she got, and she got it overnight. Now that's what I call fast action. From that day until this, I call her 'Sister Ragamuffin' to tease her, but she's not a ragamuffin any longer; she is Mrs. Collier of Boston."

Beckley: "What was the deep rooted cause of her trouble?"

Rev Ike: "Like so many other good folks she lacked self-awareness that I talk about. Because of her lack of money, she had taken to the bottle. She told me that she drank all the time. Her bills were stacking up and she had recently lost her job to top off her string of bad luck. The moral is that you must learn how to manipulate your life and I guarantee this type of thing won't happen to you."

Beckley: "But what if you just lost your job, like this woman? Isn't this going to set you back?"

Rev Ike: "It shouldn't. Losing a job is okay. That's beautiful because sometimes we're too busy holding onto the lesser, and we would

YOU CAN TAKE IT WITH YOU

never aspire to the greater. Locate something better. Put your time to better use. Don't let one person—one boss—enslave you. And it's a very simple thing to point out that the people who do get rich, they don't get rich because they work their behinds; they get rich because they work their minds."

Beckley: "Rev. Ike, you talk so positively about money. And you talk about the lack of money being the root of all evil. Yet, there seems to be in our world today a segment of society, in particular law enforcement officials and politicians, who will do anything to make a buck, even accept a bribe. All manner of corruption, usually involving finance, keeps surfacing. How

YOU CAN TAKE IT WITH YOU

do you see this as fitting into your philosophy? In these cases that I'm referring to, money has been an instrument of evil and negativity."

Rev Ike: "Anything can be used correctly or incorrectly. In my experience, I have seen the lack of money do more evil than the presence of money. It hasn't caused me to do any evil, and money certainly hasn't caused me to love the Lord less. I love the Lord a lot better riding around in a Rolls Royce than I did pawning my jacket after school to get a quarter to ride the bus home."

Beckley: "How do you account for some of the top criminals having so much wealth?"

Rev Ike: "They have the awareness for it, as far as dollars and cents figures are concerned. The Bible even says 'The Lord is no respecter of persons. The sun shines on the just and the unjust.'"

Beckley: "How do you feel about establishing a fixed income for the unfortunate in this country?"

Rev Ike: "That would be impossible. I'm amused whenever I hear the suggestion that the wealth should be equally distributed. You could distribute all of the wealth equally and tomorrow it would be back just about where it was. Here again, it's a matter of self-awareness."

YOU CAN TAKE IT WITH YOU

(**Publishers Note**: *Just as one needs to be aware of what a person will be confronted by in the "great unknown," once they have passed over into the land of the "dead," which in actually is just a new beginning.*)

"People have to be psychologically equipped to handle wealth. People who aren't couldn't handle it even if it were dumped into their laps. The only thing that fixes a person's income in our society is his self-awareness."

Beckley: "Do you also harbor negative feelings about social security, as you do about welfare programs and share-the-wealth schemes?"

Rev Ike: "Social Security I think is fine. This means that people who have worked are receiving the fruits of their labor. When it comes to welfare, I have said that welfare has its place. But it shouldn't be a resting place. I think the welfare system as it is, is especially degrading to the minorities, and in particular to the black minorities.

"The welfare system has instilled a welfare psychology in the black community. Black people think welfare is a job. And it's their job to demand more and more. They don't realize that somebody has to work, and that whatever the welfare recipient gets out of welfare, comes out of somebody's paycheck. In fact, I think

YOU CAN TAKE IT WITH YOU

welfare—after being a temporary help— becomes a form of slavery. No man is free until he becomes independent, until he is able to make his own way."

Beckley: "But how can you shut your eyes to those who aren't able to take care of themselves?"

Rev Ike: "Don't get me wrong, I'm not against charity. Charity has its place. In the in-

YOU CAN TAKE IT WITH YOU

stances where people have become disabled or something, that's different. But these cases only make up a small percentage of the welfare rolls. Let's talk about healthy, able-bodied souls. Included in the welfare system should be some definite training programs."

Beckley: "You do have some programs yourself that are attached to the church. I've heard you are helpful in rehabilitating."

Rev Ike: "That's true. We have a staff of ministers and other people who counsel youngsters with drug problems. A lot of those we've helped come back and. join the church. They tell me our training has improved their lives a hundred per cent. Re-shaped their way of thinking. They hear me talk about the presence of God within, and all of a sudden they are transformed into different individuals."

Note by Timothy Beckley: *While "unconventional," in many respects, Rev Ike's talk of God being within is affirmatively a positive way of thinking that allows for an individual to begin creating their own personal reality which will eventually benefit them when it comes to moving beyond the established gates of mortality.*

Beckley: "Do you believe the world's going to the dogs?"

Rev Ike: "It seems every generation

thinks that. They say, 'Well, things are terrible. The world's going to the dogs.' Well, hell, the world has been in the dogs—with the dogs—all the time. So negatives don't change. Neither do positives.

"But you have to decide which side you're going to be on. When Harry Truman was running for president, somebody from the opposition said, 'Oh, this inflation is terrible. Why, back in 1932 you could buy so much more with a quarter.' Truman's answer summed up pretty well. 'Sure, but who had a quarter in 1932?' "

Beckley: "You actually get into economics a bit then?"

Rev Ike: "I've tried to transmit positive ideas of success and prosperity as far and wide

YOU CAN TAKE IT WITH YOU

as possible—even to the financial community. Not too long ago we took an ad out in the **Wall Street Journal**. I wanted to bring some optimistic thinking to our captains of finance. It's just as applicable by everyone from the president to the dog catcher. Of course, you realize there has been quite a bit of despair here lately in big money circles, and when there is despair in the financial community, this affects the whole nation—and the world.

"A couple of days after the ad appeared in the paper, I got a call from the **Associated Press**. A reporter from their New York office wanted to interview me. He asked me all sorts of things. I tried to explain to him about the stock market. You see, the market is pure psychology. It's just like a nervous old woman. Everything that happens in the mass minds affects the stock market.

"The stock market is just like a widow in a windstorm. The mass awareness, and particularly the awareness of the people in the financial community, is what controls the stock market. The money people today are saying, well, that money is scarce. There isn't any money around anymore. So I asked the man from the AP, *'But where has it gone?'*

"Would you be surprised to find out it hasn't gone anywhere? The people who control the flow of our cash are sitting on it and not letting it circulate. Money hasn't gone anywhere. It's a matter of circulation. As far as the national economy is concerned, money needs to be kept in circulation. And recessions and depressions only happen when the so-called money people become nervous and begin to sit on their stacks of greenbacks."

Beckley: "But isn't it hard for the oppressed to get their hands on some of this capital?"

Rev Ike: "Nonsense. How about A.G. Gaston? He's a black businessman down in Birmingham, Alabama. A black man right down in the middle of Ku Klux Klan country. He's been a millionaire since God-knows-when. Interestingly enough, he once made a statement which I find fascinating and true to form. He said, 'Having people think that you've got money is the same as having money.' It's a known fact that people automatically give to those who have. Everyone wants to he part of a winning team.

"Them that's got are them that gets. It's a simple and basic truth that manages to elude a lot of well-meaning but unaware folks. The Bible even says. *'The Lord has hidden these things from the wise and the prudent. and revealed them unto babes.'*

Beckley: "Even though you frown on the

YOU CAN TAKE IT WITH YOU

more orthodox religions, you have adapted some of your protocol from the established churches. For example, prayer; don't you believe in praying?"

Rev Ike: "Absolutely. Here again—to me— prayer is a mental transaction rather than a conversation between somebody here on earth and somebody that's way beyond the sky. Prayer takes place within.

"Money is just one of those things. I have seen the lack of money do more evil than the presence of money. It hasn't caused me to do evil or love the Lord less. And you don't have to kneel down to pray. It all goes on in your mind."

(**Editor's Note:** *Readers should take heed that this doctrine of not having to kneel down and "beg" should be applied to our philosophy of what it takes to get a good seat in the "house of the Lord" once your last breath has been taken. You should prepare your mind for what lies ahead. Do not be afraid of death for it cannot easily be overcome, but get your mind ready to establish a beachhead on the other side.*)

Beckley: "How exactly should one go about praying to get what they want?"

Rev Ike: "The Bible tells us, 'Come boldly to the throne of grace.' Come boldly! When you pray, pray in a certain attitude. Stick your Divine chest out. Stand up in your Godship. And whatever you want, say, 'I'm worthy of this.' If it's a new home you want, say, 'I'm worthy of a new home.' If it's a better job you want, say, 'I'm worthy of a better job.' That's the way we pray in our church.

"None of this old thing, 'Lord, here I come on knee bended and body bowed in the humblest way that I know. Now, Lord, if it is your holy will... .'

"I'd never tell anybody to knee bend and body bow. In fact, the way I often put it, "if you kneel down to pray, it puts you in a position to get a swift kick in the behind." I say, "Come boldly as Jesus did when he multiplied the fish and the loaves. He just lifted up His Divine Sonship and said, 'Thank you, Father!'"

"I also tell people that anything you give thanks for, you draw it out of you into your experience. That's what multiplied the loaves and the fish for Jesus. He accepted it as already done. He sealed the bargain by saying, 'Thank you, Father!'

"If there is a God somewhere else, he couldn't have backed out. The universe can't back out of a bargain when you seal it with, 'Thank you, Father.' If you honor God-in-you, everybody else will honor God-in-you."

YOU CAN TAKE IT WITH YOU

Beckley: "We've been talking a lot about money here. I would assume you can take Rev Ike's philosophy and apply it to other of life's pressing matters, including matters of health and wellness?"

Rev Ike: "That's the approach to take. With your self-awareness, you can acquire health. And the most effective way, the absolute way to practice healing yourself or for another is for you to simply retire into your own self-awareness, and to become the very self-awareness of good health. And then you will automatically communicate that to everyone who is any part of your consciousness.

"Identify yourself with the state of health which you wish to express. This works in other areas, as you can see for yourself when you try out my philosophy. It is with the currency of self-awareness that you purchase happiness. It is with the currency of self-awareness that you purchase love.

"See yourself as the person who is loving and being loved. See yourself as love, and you will magnetize yourself to draw the right people to you for every right purpose. And the wrong people won't be able to touch you. Some people that may be even close to you now, they'll just go the other way. Let them!

"Many of those who come to the United

YOU CAN TAKE IT WITH YOU

church for guidance find it necessary to break away from former ties. Some of those who can't accept this teaching will inevitably try to drag you down. You mustn't let them!"

Beckley: "Not to put you down, but a lot of what you preach isn't that new. Your basic philosophy sounds like a cross between Christian Science, Norman Vincent Peal's positive thinking and psychic manifestation that says, what you visualize can be yours."

Rev Ike: "I don't have a patent on this. I don't profess to have a monopoly on this particular philosophy, although I do claim to be the only one preaching it to the masses. The reason for this is I've been able to bring a lot of abstracts down to a certain level of understanding—a level of understanding that is applicable to the common man in the street. Sure, our psychic powers, as such, are always at work with everyone. Each person's individual mentality is both a transmitter and receiver, psychically.

"And a person's self-awareness is always receiving and transmitting according to the nature of 'Society begins with the individual.'

"We teach the individual to come to peace with himself. Out of this inner self-decency, he will be right with his fellow man. That's why the Bible says, 'As a man thinks in his heart, so he is.' It says in Proverbs 29: 18, 'Where there is

YOU CAN TAKE IT WITH YOU

no vision, the people perish.'

(**Editor's Note**: The heart and the mind are interconnected to our everlasting images that constitute our continuation and positioning in the new world we shall be entering. Our off world existence will depend on our mental imaging. We must learn to start constructing our place of futuristic being as soon as we can and not let it wait till the last moment. *'If you can't visualize yourself in a better condition. you'll die in your poor condition. If you can't visualize yourself having money, you will die in poverty. If you can not visualize yourself being successful, you will die a dismal failure.'* Or so says Rev. Ike, and we find ourselves in complete agreement here.)

Beckley: "How do you evaluate the psychic field in general? In other words, how far do you go along with modern research such as the Russians are doing in trying to make this into a science?"

Rev Ike: "I think it's simply wonderful that people are finally finding out the power of the mind, but as far as I'm concerned it is already a science. It used to be people thought that these things were just superstitions, and now the so-called scientists are beginning to understand and utilize this power of the mind. Believe you me, within the next ten years people are going to be more into psychic phenomena and mental expansion than they have ever been. People are beginning to understand that the mind knows virtually no limits."

Beckley: "Tell me, if you were given a free hand to change the entire world picture, what would you do and how would you go about doing it?"

Rev Ike: "I'd do exactly what I'm doing now. Only I'd do more of it. I'd go on trying to teach the individual his own self-mastery, because society and the world are made up of individuals. The individual is the first unit of society. Social panaceas applied just at a mass level would never work. Because society begins with the individual. We teach the individual first to come to peace with himself. We teach him that out of this inner self-decency, he will be right with his fellow man. That's the way we will obtain peace in the world. There can be no righteousness in the world until man comes to peace within himself. Individually, that's what I'm trying to do. I wouldn't change that—it's my life's work."

YOU CAN TAKE IT WITH YOU

THERE'S NO WAY I WAS BORN TO JUST PAY MY BILLS AND DIE
By Maria D'Andrea MsD, D.D., DRH

DEDICATION

To my sons, Rob D'Andrea and Rick Holecek:

Who always walk with Higher Power, who put back whenever they can in a multitude of ways and always do their best to help others.

They walk the Path of Light.

* * * * * * * * *

FOREWORD
By Rob D'Andrea

This book has really helped me with manifesting. I already knew about the general principles on this subject, however, anytime that I tried, I did not do it the right way. So instead of doing it again half-heartedly, like before, I decided that I would read this book and manifest correctly this time. Once I read this book and began to really manifest, it became apparent within the first month that something positive was happening!

Without going into detail, I would like to just give you the gist of my experience. Since it was only the first month, I did not attribute my "good luck" to my manifesting. Only when my good fortune escalated over the next several months did I realize that "luck" did not have anything to do with this. The timing of results varies, but it is definitely a reality to start seeing results as quickly as I did. Although I have not fully reached my goals as of yet, I am much closer than I would have been. I have even added to my manifesting list of goals. Besides working hard at it, and trying everything that I can, this book has given me a huge edge on acquiring my goals.

Of course, the main thrust of this book has as much to do with processing the "new world" we are going to go to when we die, as it has to do in the here and now. Thus, I am unable — thank goodness! — to comment on this aspect of my mom's work — or the noble work of the other contributors — but I think her approach to the after life is pretty much on the mark.

YOU CAN TAKE IT WITH YOU

Thus, you can bet I strongly recommend this book to anyone who is even remotely interested in the paranormal and I urge you to give it a serious try. Do not become discouraged if results are not immediate. The timing of manifesting goals varies but you must stay consistent and keep at it. The metaphysical realm works in the best possible way for us and in the most positive way that we need. Even though we prefer immediate results, please keep this book as a reference for down the road. I can promise you that you will not regret it.

YOUR LIFE HERE AND IN THE BEYOND

Many of us as shaman, mystics, and psychics among other practitioners of the mystical/magickal arts know that in the afterlife, there is so much abundance, that you can take it with you.

Whatever your belief system is, when you look into it, you will find it speaks of a reward of some sort once you shed your earthy physical form. And why not?

Whatever you call the next phase of existence, heaven, overworld, etheric world or any other label, it is still the same. It is a place of joy and abundance in the next realm.

I see it as a soul who is now in a new re-

YOU CAN TAKE IT WITH YOU

fined etheric frequency. Once on the other side, the person is in a realm which vibrates at a different rate than our physical world. Nonetheless, it is just as real.

God (or whatever you chose to personally call the Source) wants us to be happy; not only happy in this life but also the next. As humans we tend to limit our outlook. We know there is a "Heaven," but also we've always heard that you can't take it with you. We can't take the physical aspects with us, such as money or a house, but we certainly can take our rewards with us.

I look at the next realm as being on the etheric plane and not so much "above" us, as in a different time and space. When you pass into the next realm, you usually first land in a place that you expect.

If you expect mansions, that is what you will see. Once you learn to navigate in your new

YOU CAN TAKE IT WITH YOU

environment, you can have all the abundance you desire. There aren't any limits except the limits of your imagination. Your soul will feel free and non-limited.

You can go to other planets, various destinations or simply stay in a place you chose and have people around you that you love.

You as a non-physical being will be unlimited. Some look at the ethericplane as a place with many rooms, some look at it as various levels. The concept is that the better you behave in this realm of the physical existence, the more your reward. If you helped others from the heart and were loving in how you dealt with them, your reward will be greater than someone who was negative and mean in their dealings with others.

The other dimensions react to our energies. As an example: someone who demonstrated charity and kindness, will be in a happy, wonderful realm. This is because there is a metaphysical, occult law that states "Like Attracts Like."

This doesn't mean that once on the other side, you can't reevaluate your past and decide that you have learned your lesson. Then explore your new surroundings and now manifest your new abundance.

YOU CAN TAKE IT WITH YOU

Even though they say you can't take money with you, that doesn't mean that you can't create all the abundance you desire. Why put limits on a non-limited plane of existence?

As a shaman and psychic, I've seen some of the other realms. When I ask a soul who passed on to come to me, I get different scenarios. Some are in a place of learning, some in a city, and some in a place that I can't really see. But they are happy and joyful and feel free. So I've named it their Happy Place, wherever each soul happens to be.

When my mother was close to passing away, she told me she saw a big party ship docked by the shore, with a man holding a boarding ledger waiting for her to get on the ship to check off her name. She was walking down a street between buildings, looking happy as she was walking toward it. She could hear the music. She wanted to make sure the ship waited for her and could see people celebrating and dancing (she loved to dance) and waiting for her. When she did "leave," I saw her soul body lift up, smile and go toward the ship happily.

To repeat, everyone has their what I call "Happy Place" to which they go and "retire" from their life on earth.

There is a Native American tribe that be-

YOU CAN TAKE IT WITH YOU

lieves that once you pass on, you get into a canoe. You paddle upriver until you see the teepees of your loved ones. There you get out of the canoe and you can hunt, fish and be happy all the time.

God doesn't want you to be poor in this life or the next. There is a Higher Kingdom. Now, I'm not saying that I'm in any rush to get there. But, when it is my time, I know that I can be happy, abundant and free from limitations. That is why we don't have fear. We are simply moving on to a different vibrational realm and a new adventure.

HOW TO TAKE IT ALONG WITH YOU

Some simple rituals help you to attain what you decide to manifest in both realities. So let's do one for abundance.

1. Get a white candle of any size.

2. Anoint it with Success Oil or High John Oil while focusing on a positive thought.

3. Wear something white. It can be a small piece of material, a shirt, etc.

4. Next, sit comfortably with the candle in front of you. Take 3 slow, deep breaths to relax. Light the candle and say 3 times:

By the Power of three times three,
Divine Protection comes to me.

YOU CAN TAKE IT WITH YOU

And as I say, so shall it be.

5. Now, focus your mind and visualize–

The abundance you are creating in your life. . .

Then, what you can do to help others.

6. Do these until you feel you are finished. Put out the candle (do NOT blow on it). Throw any remainder of the candle outside your house and walk away.

The focus on what you can do for others creates a "deposit" into your ethereal bank, as long as you are sincere.

VOYAGING RITUAL

Sit somewhere comfortable and relax. You are going on an exciting new voyage.

Visualize yourself with your eyes closed, on the shore of a lush green meadow with a beautiful blue, calm river.

You are standing next to a boat (you pick what type of boat, what it is made of, possibly a color or ornamentation and so forth).

Next to you, on the shore, is a big purple bag. It looks very full. Open the bag and pull out all the things that you want now and to take with you to the next realm. Pull out the items or symbols of what you will take such as a heart symbol for love and so on.

YOU CAN TAKE IT WITH YOU

Place each into the boat, one at a time. When you have put everything you desire into the boat, close the bag and leave it where it is.

You can always come back and add more.

Visualize yourself being happy with your choices and slowly open your eyes. You are now prepared for years down the road when you take your last journey to your "Happy Place," and can forget about it.

CREATE YOUR FUTURE

God does not want you to suffer in silence. He wants you to live a prosperous life in the here and now and in the by and by.

I have a saying I came up with for my students in the spiritual/metaphysical/paranormal fields:

You don't have to believe it, to create it!

You simple have to put the thought out to the universe in order to manifest a good job, wealth, love or anything you decide to focus on as your goal.

I came up with a way to explain how to manifest by using the word: "TAP." This is how it works:

Think of a triangle. At the left bottom corner is the word "Thought," at the point at the top is the word "Astral," and at the right bottom corner is "Physical" = TAP. First you put out in your Thought what you focus on as your intent to bring in, that thought goes to the Astral plane where it forms and comes back down to the Physical realm to manifest and become a physical reality.

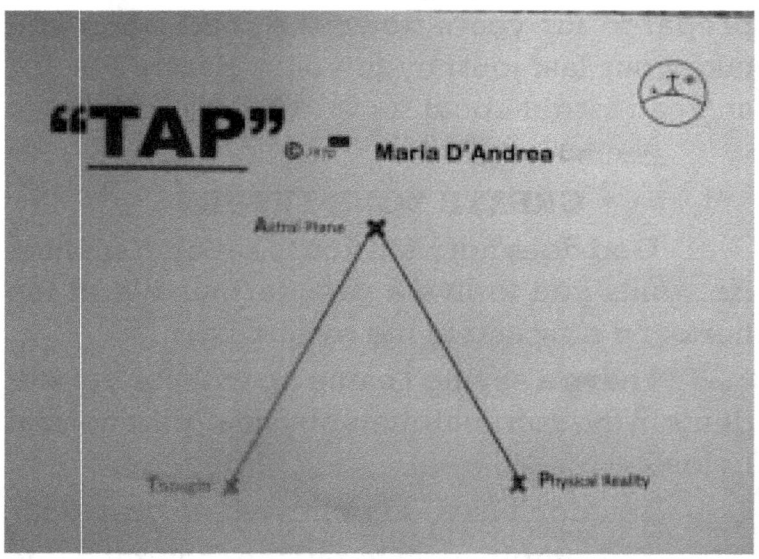

We have all known people who say — I always have a headache—and why are they surprised when they do? Nobody else is surprised they have one. The universe is very exact. So all you have to do is just put your goals out there.

Now, let's get down to the real manifesting. There are some basic steps that you need to be aware of to accomplish your goals.

You have to have a plan.

YOU CAN TAKE IT WITH YOU

You have to do only positive.

You have to have focus.

You have to "know/trust" it is coming in.

You have to have a positive outlook.

You have to give back in some form.

You have to say Thank You when it "hits."

We are not meant to suffer in silence. We are the children of God/Our Source—use whatever your name is for that Source. (Put in your own term for your Source, because that is what will resonate with your belief system and energy.) If our Source is unlimited and we are the children of that Source, how can we not be abundant and successful in everything we decide to do? It is because we forgot who we are. WE are co-creators.

We are unlimited but in a limiting world of concepts. We have to remember who we are. We have free will to decide what path we wish to go on. You are at a crossroad or you wouldn't be reading this book. You know within yourself that all things are possible; you simply needed a reminder and an outline on how to get there. Think of this as being on a path and looking at the road map to get to your destination.

I work full time in the spiritual fields, as a public speaker on the subjects, among other connected fields. Not one is a definite income,

YOU CAN TAKE IT WITH YOU

yet I have never even been late paying a bill. I know that it will be paid and it always is. I've owned houses and people don't understand how I can do all this without a 9-5 job. Once you see results, you get used to it and it becomes automatic to expect it to work. I never question it because I know it does work. It can work for you too.

Are you going to choose the path of abundance and wealth or the path where you are struggling daily? You need to shake things up. Change the way you are dealing and start on the path to abundance. You can do it. Go ahead, take that first step… Go on…I know you can…

WORKING GOD'S PLAN FOR YOU

First things first. You need to understand how it all works so that you can work the plan.

You Have To Pick A Goal
In Any Area Of Your Life.

I suggest starting with a material goal. Now, some people will tell you that money is evil. These people are limiting their abundance just by believing in that thought, and so they are creating lack. Money isn't evil, the love of money is negative, because that means the person is putting money before family, friends and

YOU CAN TAKE IT WITH YOU

all else.

Think about this: the more money/wealth you have, the more people you can help. You can help them if they need food (takes money to buy it), you can give them a ride if they have to get to work and their car has a flat (you need money to own a car so you can give them a lift) and so on. Who are you going to help if you are broke and don't have anything? You would be too busy working on survival. That's not for us.

God knows your name and promised that you would have a good life. You simply need to stick to the plan to get you there.

You Have To Learn To Do Only Do Positive Things.

We all know you can't always be positive, because we deal with other people in our daily lives. But do the best you can. You have to have your own ethics, and your own spiritual belief system. You know what is right or wrong so stick with it.

We harm none. We put out positive to attract positive. There's a spiritual law that states "like attracts like." If someone is negative, how is that person going to attract the raise they feel they deserve or the promotion they are looking forward to? How are they going to win at the lottery if they are negative and taking someone else's money.

GOD TAKES CARE OF HIS OWN!

I knew this gentleman who was my client who came to me for readings. One day he found a wallet on the street. Obviously someone lost it and was going to be very upset. Some would have ignored it or taken the money and not returned it. My client picked up the wallet, opened it and found contact information in it. He proceeded to get in touch with the man who lost it. He didn't touch the money. The man came and fully expected the money to be missing. He was very grateful and thanked my client for all the trouble he had gone through. He then explained that it was the money to pay a very important bill. He offered my client some restitution for all his time and for going out of his way. My client didn't take anything, but was happy to help. He did the right thing and God – or the universe if you are a humanist and not religious – would later rember this and pay my client back ten fold.

A few weeks later, he found a lottery ticket on the street. He thought he would check if it was a winning ticket and sure enough, it was! He didn't win millions, but it did win a little over a thousand dollars and the ticket was free. The universe was "paying" him back. You never know what form this "payback" will take—and it often does come unexpectedly. But that's the way it works my friends.

You Have To Have Focus.

If you don't focus on a goal, how will the universe know what you really want instead of all the stray thoughts we normally have?

Focus on your intent. Take 10-15 minutes each day. I suggest the first thing in the morning and the last thing prior sleep. Or pick a time that works for you.

Put your feelings and emotions behind it. If you can't feel it and get excited about it, how will the universe act on it? It's like having an extra battery charger when you do that.

Do this consistently for three weeks and I can almost guarantee that you can count on a long lasting resolution that will reach over into the afterlife.

Next, Trust. Let It Go And Forget About It.

You "know" your Source is on it. God hasn't forgotten you. It will come in the right time. You can count on the outcome.

You have to have trust and just know it is manifesting in your favor.

YOU CAN TAKE IT WITH YOU

Think of it this way: If your earthly father went to the store with you and you asked him for candy, he would say - yes, before we leave the store I will get it for you. You would say thank you and go about your business, knowing that before you leave, he will buy the candy. He already said yes, so you expect it and know you are getting it.

It is the same way with your Source. Once you focus your intent and expect it to come to fruition, it will. Think of how unlimited your Source is. Anything you can conceive, manifest and work on in the physical world, you can receive.

Get excited! Yay. Woohoo. You are steadfastly reaching your goal.

I'm always saying - I Go Direct.

One of my clients' years ago started saying IGD. So I asked him what that is and he said, "I GO Direct." You would think I would have known that. Figures, right?

You can tell when someone is working what I refer to as "The Plan." This is when a person "knows" and "trusts" in the outcome. You will actually see the proof in the pudding.

They will have no fear. They will not be stressed. They will not worry. They will demonstrate calmness and trust.

YOU CAN TAKE IT WITH YOU

They will go about the physical work, such as job hunting or going to a healer of some kind, but they will go about it with inner calm, knowing that this attitude will probably benefit them for time immortal.

It all comes down to *do you trust in your Source or not?*

Put your focus on your Source — God/Divine Power — and the ultimate outcome, not what is going on now. If you are in a negative situation now, do the physical groundwork. Look for that job, but do not stress. However, get excited about the new opportunity, because it is coming your way.

If your job is folding, know that a better one on the way. If you can't pay the rent, just know that the money will soon be coming in. If your car is not working right, you will find the right mechanic or receive a better or come across a sweetheart deal on another vehicle. The Source always moves you upward.

A few years ago, I had a beautiful car that I was leasing. It had to be turned in soon, and I wasn't sure what to do next. I didn't want to lease again and make payments on a car I didn't own. I didn't want to get a new car, because I didn't want to make more payments. I go to car shows at times because I like the older cars and I used to go with my mother who was knowledgeable about them. I decided I wanted an older car that was fun and as she pointed out at the shows, my insurance would also go down.

So I was at peace, expecting the unexpected, as usual. I had no idea how it would happen, but I knew it would. It always works. We should never question the ways of the "Master."

It happened to be around my birthday and I still had the leased car. My birthday came and a wonderful gentleman gave me a Monte Carlo SS that was older (knowing I wanted an older car). It was genuinely a surprise. Who would have thought of that? So when I had to turn in my car, I already had one to switch to. You can't make this stuff up.

We are not working hard on gaining wealth, money, prosperity, healing, love or abundance. When we know, trust and are doing the Plan, then it will come. You are only working on that part. That is your part of the job. Stay in calmness and peace. People will not understand why you aren't stressed, but you will know why.

It is as though you have awakened.

Hold Onto That Positive Outlook.

Stay positive. Don't focus on the negative. Don't think— it's been a week already, where is

YOU CAN TAKE IT WITH YOU

what I have been trying to manifest? Put your trust in the higher nature of the universe and everything will be alright.

If you find yourself thinking negative thoughts about the situation or about anything else, you have to reverse it.

The more positive we are in our daily lives, the quicker things will come our way. We are attracting a higher spiritual vibration thus becoming more in sync with universal energies. We are bettering our lives. We are adding to the strength of that cosmic magnet in our souls that will pull abdundance headon into our aura.

We always hear about how some people think if you are born into a rich family, you will have wealth. As in - money goes to money. The truth is that It's not their inheritance; but their outlook. They grew up expecting money and wealth, therefore attracting it.

The universal rule—God's rule — change your outlook, change your life!

So if you find yourself having doubts about anything or having a negative thought, mentally or verbally say the word "CANCEL" and substitute a positive thought. Some days I'm going cancel, cancel, cancel... After all, we are human.

So as an example: if you find yourself

YOU CAN TAKE IT WITH YOU

thinking, "What if I can't make my next bill?" Well just say "Cancel." Then say, "Of course my bills will get paid effortlessly. I always achieve this or better. God is in my corner."

We Always Put Back.

We always put back. Life is a circle. We give, we take, we give...

Do you get the idea?

People misunderstand at times, what giving back means. They assume it means only money, such as tithing. First of all, tithing isn't just money, it's giving back in many other forms. This is one of those big misunderstandings that can set us back.

The important part is that we are all connected. As a European shaman, we look at it as if we are all part of a gigantic spider web. On this web you have each soul on a strand of it. When one soul/person moves and shakes the web, it affects everyone on that web.

So to give back means it has to be from the heart. If you give because you are expecting a result from it or something back, it won't work. If you are giving back because you want to, then it counts.

We all need money in this physical realm and deserve it. You heard me, right? You de-

YOU CAN TAKE IT WITH YOU

serve it. You are a spiritual being living in a physical body, at least temporarily. As a Higher being you should not be limited by earthy thoughts or things. Go get that money. Go get that job that brings it. Go for a business you never thought you could do. Remember who you are and that you are unlimited. For truly, God wants you to thrive. It proves He has the vast capacity to pull us through any situation.

You have to be Prosperity Conscious. God wants you to be happy. How can that be if you let your thoughts drag you down like quicksand into lack instead of wealth?

Give Thanks Twice.

We always say thank you. The energy of doing so is a form of payment to the spirit realms.

YOU CAN TAKE IT WITH YOU

After all, didn't you say thank you to your father for the candy? So you say thanks for the help in gaining wealth or obtaining other goals.

Say "thank you" when you first start to focus on your desires. After all, as you ask so will you receive. It is already coming to you. Next, say thanks when you receive your "reward." You are paying the universe with love energy and it will return the favor whether you realize it or not.

THERE IS NO END TO THE RAINBOW

Yes, there's gold at the end of the rainbow or another way to say it is, you've reached your goal.

YAY! Now what? Now, you can set yet another higher goal. At this point you already know you can do it.

Suppose you started manifesting that you gain higher pay in your job? Now, you've achieved that. You may decide that your next goal is to have a promotion to a higher position which comes with an even higher salary. Go for it.

Learn to never limit yourself.

If you don't know how to make more money because your job may be limiting, have as your goal having a certain amount of money

YOU CAN TAKE IT WITH YOU

each week, month or year in a positive way, consistently, in a way/job/business that you like and will be good at it. The reason you must be happy is because if you hate the job, eventually you will quit. The reason for you being good at it is, so they appreciate your ability and want to keep you and thus you build your self-esteem. Not ego, but self-esteem.

Don't cancel yourself out by thinking you can't achieve a goal. Don't go by what others say that might limit you. Don't tell others what your goal is unless they are really supportive. You don't want their thoughts to slow you down. You can always tell them after you've achieved your goal. They don't understand you aren't limited. You are only as limited as your thoughts are limited. Wealthy thoughts create wealthy situations.

STARTING A NEW LIFE OF ABUNDANCE

You may say that you've never been able to achieve making major money in the past. That has nothing to do with today. Today you are starting a new, abundant, prosperous life. Know it is so. It is. You are taking your first step into your great, exciting future. Look forward to it. See in your mind what you will do with your wealth. Where will you spend it? Who you can help?

YOU CAN TAKE IT WITH YOU

Wealth gives you freedom. It gives you the freedom to have time to help others, to accomplish more. You will have more time with your family and friends and to enjoy your life more. The more you have, the more you can assist those in your life that you favor.

Look at famous people who have wealth. They are philanthropists. Not because of tax breaks, but because they know that giving back from the heart creates more wealth. As you put it out it comes back Ten Fold. Many do so anonymously because they aren't looking for earthly appreciation, they are simply following the "Law of Ten Fold."

Today is the start of your new manifesting. We learn from the past, start creating today and reap the rewards of it in the future. So we are not moving backward, but we are moving always (all ways) forward.

As you become more and more in sync

YOU CAN TAKE IT WITH YOU

with universal energies and become a higher and higher spiritual being, you will take that abundant spiritual outlook and understanding with you into your next life. You will be transported to a higher—loftier—position in Heaven in accordance to the behavior pattern you established while still stationed here.

Life is a great adventure. Enjoy it. Ride the wave of prosperity.

Get excited! Go ahead! You know you want to. You are under your own control. Set your sights higher. Once you've achieved that, set the new goal even higher. Think of climbing a ladder one rung at a time. You cannot fail or fall. God has your back. He is on your side.

And so my dear friend, remember: **You Can Take It With You** in addition to having all you want in the here and now!

YOU CAN TAKE IT WITH YOU

MARIA WOULD LIKE TO SPEAK PERSONALLY WITH YOU!

CONTACT MARIA D' ANDREA FOR...

READINGS
Private by Phone/Mail/In Person

*

WORKSHOPS

*

SEMINARS

*

BOOKS AND PRODUCTS

*

MAIL ORDER COURSES

Contact Maria D'Andrea at:
Mailing address:
PO BOX 52
Mineola, NY 11501
Offices on Long Island and Manhattan

Phone: (631) 559-1248

Email: maria@mariadandrea.com

PayPal: mdandrea100@gmail.com

YOU CAN TAKE IT WITH YOU

FINDING HEAVEN'S POT OF GOLD
Sir L. J. Baldry

PREFACE

Getting rich, and remaining rich, is really NOT a matter of "Luck" or "Accident." Rather, it stems from the application, wittingly or unwittingly, of certain potent and often little-known financial laws.

When these laws are applied, in the manner described in this book, they cannot help but bring to you the financial and other riches you so rightly deserve in life!

Yes, you may 'accidentally' become rich, such as when someone dies and leaves you money or when you win a large money prize in a lottery or other game of chance. But remaining rich? That, certainly, is another matter alto-

YOU CAN TAKE IT WITH YOU

gether!

The Rich of this world became rich, and remain rich, by knowingly or unknowingly (usually the former) applying all or most of the financial laws set down in this book.

Like them, apply these Laws in your daily life and see your financial circumstances improve beyond your wildest dreams!

YOU CAN TAKE IT WITH YOU

Chapter One
THE LAW OF MENTAL IMAGERY
Definition:

The Law of Mental Imagery, simply put, states that whatever situation, condition or circumstances you regularly, persistently and faithfully imagine yourself to be in WILL ultimately come to pass in physical reality.

In other words, this Law states that you ultimately become whatever you persistently imagine yourself to be. That is, if you, deliberately or otherwise, make it a practice to imagine yourself in poor, miserable conditions you will, in the future, undoubtedly experience those very same conditions in your life. On the other hand, if you unrelentingly imagine yourself as being rich and happy you will, whatever your present financial circumstances, be rich and happy in the future.

YOU CAN TAKE IT WITH YOU

YOUR MIND IS A VERITABLE GOLDMINE!

Whatever images you habitually form and hold in your mind will be materialized in the physical world. Your mind is a most powerful and complex 'instrument' which, when used in a certain way, will most assuredly bring your innermost desires into physical reality. If you are poor, commence to form and retain mental images of yourself in rich and happy circumstances; if you are already comfortably off financially you must, nevertheless, picture yourself (in your mind) in richer and happier circumstances. Persevere in forming and holding these mental images and your future financial prosperity is assured. Hold onto your menial pictures faithfully and diligently, and you will make astounding financial progress sooner than you currently think possible.

KAREN FULFILLS HER AMBITION

Ever since Karen D. left high school in her native New York City, USA, she worked very hard towards her deep-seated desire to become a fashion model—not just any model but a well-known, well-paid model. Karen had the burning desire, and was prepared to work very hard to accomplish her objective. What Karen needed was the right opportunities, the right doors to be opened, for her to achieve her aim.

But coming as she did from a poor financial background Karen understood all too well that entry into and, more importantly, success in, the highly competitive world of modelling would not come easily. She knew that New York City, like any other major city, was 'filled' with young beautiful women who wanted to become sucessful models. Would she, she wondered again and again, be able to make it as a model, a successful model?

During her last year at high school, Karen learnt from one of her female teachers a secret that was later to change her life completely: the secret that whatever you regularly and persistently imagine yourself to be will, sooner or later, come true in actuality.

Cheryl L., the teacher in question, was very fond of Karen, who was easily the best student in the history class she taught. Cheryl, frequently chatted with the pretty young girl after normal class hours. One day she casually asked Karen: "Tell me, Karen, what work will you do when you grow up?"

'Aw, I'm already grown up!" replied Karen, giggling as she said so.

"I mean when you really grow up," persisted Cheryl.

"I'll love to be a top-class model," answered Karen, her face taking on a more serious look.

"You know, " Karen continued, shyly staring at the ground, "that has been my secret ambition for a very long time now. But I suppose it will remain nothing but a dream; who would want a girl like me to model anything for them, anyway?," she concluded, tossing her long blond hair from side to side and trying very hard not to look at the elder woman.

Cheryl was deeply moved. This girl obviously possessed the looks and the ambition to become what she wanted to become in the future but, sadly, her thinking was wrong, very wrong. Unless the ridiculous idea that Karen had planted in her mind, the idea that she could not become a successful model, was removed and replaced, hers would, indeed, become only a pipe dream, leaving her unhappy, frustrated and bitter about her failure to attain her main objective in life.

"Oh, I see that you've been watching too much television," said Cheryl teasingly, putting her arm around Karen's shoulder. "But what'll you want to model?" she questioned probingly.

"Fashionable clothes, jewelery, and in-

YOU CAN TAKE IT WITH YOU

deed anything if the price is right," Karen answered.

"Hmmm!," sighed Cheryl, pleasantly surprised at this girl's obvious determination. Cheryl, therefore, gave her the Secret, the Secret that had helped her and several other persons the world over to achieve their financial and other goals in life.

Briefly, this is what Cheryl asked Karen to do:

a) For a few minutes every day (and night) she should sit or lie down comfortably, relax and imagine that she had already become the top-class model she so desperately wanted to be. She should, in her mind, see herself surrounded by wealth and all the good things that money can buy. Karen should, Cheryl insisted, form and hold those mental pictures of herself (as a successful, rich, well-known mod- el) faithfully. She should believe that the pictures would come to pass. "Remember," Cheryl added, "what Napoleon Bonaparte once said: 'Imagination rules the world' ".

(b) Take the appropriate measures to move positively in the directon of her ultimate objective. Karen should, Cheryl advised, enroll in a modelling course at a college or fashion school when she completed her high school studies. She should study very hard, all the time holding fast and faithfully to the mental images she had formed.

(c) Karen must, Cheryl emphasized, persevere in holding onto her mental images of what she ultimately wanted to be. If she did as advised, Cheryl assured, herdesires will ultimately come true. Progress may seem slow but it surely would lead Karen to her ultimate objective so long as she remained faithful to her mental images.

Karen took Cheryl's advice and subsequently enrolled in a modelling course in a local institution, attending classes on a part-time basis. Her mother disapproved, as she had wanted Karen to proceed to college after high school, but her dad gave her all the support he could.

And did she really imagine herself as a successful model? Did Karen really work hard at her lessons in the modelling institution!? Everyday and night, she would spend a few minutes seeing herself, in her mind, as having already become a high-class, highly-paid model; she would see herself, still in her mind, surrounded by opulence. Karen worked very hard at her lessons. She frequently bought and read fashion magazines, paying particular attention

YOU CAN TAKE IT WITH YOU

to information about the current top-class fashion models, the way they lived, their preferences in food, clothes and men, etc. She even cut out, from glossy magazines, the pictures of her favourite models and stuck them on a wall in her bedroom, where she could see them frequently.

Did Karen ultimately achieve her objective? Yes, she did. She successfully passed through the modelling course and moved gradually but steadily up the ladder of modelling success.

Today, Karen is one of the most highly paid models in New York City ("Karen D.," of course, is not her real name, which is being withheld to protect her identity)! She models for well-known fashion houses; she poses (not in the nude) for photographers and even painters, fashion magazines, and even frequently does television commercials. You might have, especially if you live in the New York area, seen her on television advertising one product or another. Furthermore, her face appears frequently on the covers of prestigious fashion magazines.

Does Karen have abundant money? Does she possess plenty of clothes? Karen has so many expensive clothes, so many pairs of shoes and other footwear, so much jewellery, so much money, so much glamour, so much as to make

YOU CAN TAKE IT WITH YOU

most women turn green with envy!

"Oh, she'd just been lucky," you may say; but the truth is that she has not been any luckier than you've been! All Karen did was to use her mind positively; by unrelentingly seeing herself as a successful, well-to-do person, by seeing herself surrounded by wealth in its various manifestations, and by working hard towards her goals she attained her innermost desires. YOU, of course, can do likewise and achieve your financial and other goals in life!

WHY JEREMY A. ACHIEVED BUSINESS SUCCESS

People who have known Jeremy A. for a long time wonder how he has managed to become so successful, so financially secure!

Jeremy, who lives in London, owns a number of printing businesses which are very profitable. Years ago, Jeremy owned a single printing enterprise which, year after year, only managed a little profit. But all this was soon to change for the better.

During conversation, many years ago, I pointed out to Jeremy that what seemed to be wrong was his thinking. I explained to him that if he regularly and persistently fed his mind with thoughts and images about wealth, business

YOU CAN TAKE IT WITH YOU

success, and so on, his subconscious mind could not, ultimately, help but translate his thoughts and mental images into their material equivalents.

So what did Jeremy do? Each morning he would wake up about thirty minutes earlier than he previously used to do and spent several minutes imagining that his business had expanded, that he had opened several branches not only in London but in several other cities in the UK. He imagined that he employed several well-qualified, dedicated staff. In his mind, every morning after awaken-ing from sleep and every night just before going to bed, Jeremy "saw" that his business had boomed, that he was financially secure, that he was surrounded by opulence and happiness. He struck to these mental images and, not too long after he first commenced working on his mind, his business boomed.

Suffice it to say that today he is very rich and possesses all the material symbols of wealth. Jeremy would be the first to tell you that he worked hard at his mental imagery exercises, that he hated waking up in the morning to do his imagery exercises. But he would be quick to add that those mental imagery exercises did pay off financially. Do you need a free ride around town in Jeremy's shiny Rolls-Royce

YOU CAN TAKE IT WITH YOU

before you begin to believe his story? I hope not!

THE STEPS YOU SHOULD FOLLOW

The steps which Jeremy and Karen (in the earlier story) followed are set out, in chronological order, below. It is highly recommended that you ,as much as possible, follow the same steps:

a) Decide what you want to be, what you want to do. In other words, set for yourself specific objectives before commencing to apply your mind to help you to attain these objectives.

Whatever occupational or professional objectives you decide on, it is certain that you wish to attain a position of wealth ultimately.

(b) If you can, obtain information about persons who, at the present time, enjoy the occupational/professional or financial positions you aspire to. Aim your sights very high: obtain information and, if possible, newspaper or magazine cuttings both of information about, and pictures of such persons. Look at these from time to time, as well as at newer information and pictures which appear in newspapers and magazines.

c) Find some time, early in the morning soon after you awake and at night before you

YOU CAN TAKE IT WITH YOU

go to bed, to perform the simple menial imagery exercises described below. Please note that it is most important that you adhere to the performance of these exercises.

It is of no use to start performing them this week, abandon them during the following two weeks, revert to them in the third week, and so on. Be consistant. Persevere in their performance, for it is only then that success will come to you. And please note that success will mean more money in your pocket, it could mean greater happiness in your life. What, then, are these exercises?

(d) Each morning and night (and afternoon, if you can find the time) sit or lie down comfortably. It is normally better to sit rather than lie down, since you could easily fall asleep in the latter position. Having previously ensured that there is no loud or other distracting noise about, stretch out your legs and hands, placing the palm of the left hand on your left leg and that of the right hand on the right leg and making certain that neither the legs nor the hands touch each other. Close your eyes and take in a deep breath. Hold the breath for a few seconds while saying, in your mind, the number "20".

Then, slowly, breathe out. Say the word "Relax" in your mind as you breathe out. Breathe in again, this time saying the number

YOU CAN TAKE IT WITH YOU

"19" in your mind as you hold your breath; then breathe out again, saying "Relax" in your mind as you previously did. Keep counting down from 20 until you reach zero or nought (0). Somewhere along the line, if you breathe in and out as recommended, you will notice a warm tingling sensation in your body, especially in your hands and feet. This merely indicates you are conducting the breathing exercise properly.

After counting down to zero, imagine (in your mind and with your eyes still closed) that you are beside a lake with placid, deep-blue waters. If you have seen such a lake, or other mass of water with a calm, soothing appearance then recall that relaxing experience. If you have never seen such an expanse of water before, then, by looking at pictures or paintings depicting a similar scenery, you can imagine as required.

See, then, yourself beside the lake with the beautiful, calm waters. Let your mind rest on the scenery, drinking deep of its beauty; let your mind dwell on the calm waters; with your mind's eye, clearly 'see' the waters. Let your mind be focused in this way for a few minutes, say ten minutes (or more, if you have enough time on your hands).

Then, switch your mind off from the lake with the placid waters and onto yourself. In your

YOU CAN TAKE IT WITH YOU

mind, see yourself as having already accomplished the financial, professional and other goals you have set for yourself. In other words, see yourself as having already attained your life's objectives. See yourself, in your mind, surrounded by wealth, by opulence; see yourself doing the things you love to do when you do become rich, when you do attain your objectives.

Vividly see, in your mind, the house you would wish to live in when you become rich, its furnishings, and other material possessions you would wish to have in your future home. See yourself driving your dream car; see yourself visiting the places—top restaurants, five-star hotels (if you haven't ever been to such places and other places then either pay a visit to any of them in your city or, if you can't, look at pictures of them), etc.—that you would wish to visit when your finances do improve.

Focus your mind in this way for as long as you can manage; fifteen to thirty minutes should be appropriate, although you may extend it to three-quarters of an hour if you wish. At the end of that time, open your eyes and sit quietly for about a minute before you get up to go about your normal business.

It is very important, I must repeat, that you perform the mental imagery exercises given here regularly, persistently. Endeavour to do it every day and night, wherever you are; positive results will surely come to you provided you persevere in the performance of the imagery exercises. You will find, as you continue with your exercises, that you attract towards you the people with the ideas, money, etc, to help you reach your goals. Opportunities will come your way in abundance and it is up to you to seize such opportunities when they do come. When you get a recurring idea, when the 'small voice' within you persistently tells you to take a certain business action, go to see a particular person for business advice or discussion, etc, act on this intuition.

(e) Keep doing your mental imagery exercises regularly and unrelentingly, and the things you wish for cannot help but gravitate towards you. The secret of success in this regard is to sustain your mental pictures by regular performance of the above-described mental imagery exercise.

RODNEY K. WINS THE TOP JOB

Today, Rodney K. has the job he has always wanted to have: chief executive of a medium-sized footwear producing firm in Wellington, New Zealand.

YOU CAN TAKE IT WITH YOU

When it became known that the current chief executive was scheduled to retire within the next year, nobody seemed certain who would succeed him. Apart from Rodney, there were at least three other men who possessed the practical experience, the academic qualifications and, from all appearances, the diligence, to suceed the outgoing chief executive.

Rodney wanted the job badly but he was aware that there were other contenders for the same post. This is what Rodney did:

a) Starting from the day he learnt about the imminent retirement of the current job occupant, he would sit down, morning and night, relax, and picture himself (in his mind, that is) in the chief executive's office. Having been to the big man's office several times in the course of his normal duties, Rodney was aware of the general layout of the room as well as the small details like the position of the chair, table and so on. He would, regularly and persistently, mentally picture himself seated at the big executive table, sitting on the big man's swivel chair. He "saw" his own dear name written on the name-plate on the table. He remained faithful to his mental images.

(b) Still in his mind, Rodney saw his wife, Judy, hug and kiss him happily, then he heard her congratulate him on his appointment to the post of chief executive. Similarly, he saw their two teenage children hug him and heard them congratulate him. He heard his friends phone or go personally to his house to congratulate him on his appointment as Chief Executive.

(c) Finally, Rodney saw himself enjoying the usual company perks reserved for the chief executive. For example, he saw himself being driven around town, on business, in the big company car normally used only by the chief executive.

Quite soon, all the contenders for the post submitted formal applications for consideration by the company's board of directors. They all attended interviews as required.

Several other people were surprised—most of them pleasantly—(but not Rodney) when the appointment was made: Rodney had got the top job!

IMPORTANT POINTS TO NOTE

1. You become whatever you habitually imagine yourself to be. Whatever mental pictures you form and retain, over a long period, will undeniably come to pass.

2. If you habitually focus your mind on thoughts about wealth, if you regularly and persistently imagine yourself surrounded by

YOU CAN TAKE IT WITH YOU

wealth, you cannot help but get rich ultimately.

3. The converse, of course, is true. If you habitually imagine yourself surrounded by poverty, poverty will ultimately come into your life , even if you are not currently poor.

4. Decide what professional, financial and other goals you wish to accomplish in life, for it is only YOU who knows what you want, what will make you happy. Having decided what you want, what you want to be or possess, regularly and persistently, imagine (by the process decribed elsewhere above) that you have ALREADY attained those very goals.

5. It is important that you persevere in the performance of your mental imagery exercises. In other words, stick to the mental images you have formed about what you want to be or what you want to possess ultimately. DON'T give them up even when your progress towards those ends seems slow.

6.Your MIND has power, so much power that you can't even begin to realize the full extent of its awesome powers. You will, I know, benefit tremendously if you read the book **"The Goldmine on Your Shoulders,**" published by Finbarr International, which will greatly help you in your quest for financial prosperity.

Chapter 2
THE LAW OF TITHING
Definition:

The Law of Tithing states that the person who regularly and faithfully gives a proportion of his or her income to help in the Work of God is, to say the least, assured of financial progress in life.

WHAT IS TITHING?

The word "Tithe," which is an old English word that is now out of common usage, means "Tenth." Thus, simply translated, a "tithe of your income" means one-tenth of your income, whether such income is seen in terms of cash, stocks and bonds, or other forms of material wealth.

Tithing is a system which the Lord God,

the Creator, has set down for financing His Work (ministry) on earth; it is a system which has been in existence since the days of the great Hebrew patriarchs Abraham, Isaac, Jacob, and even before their time, right through the Mosaic era until the time of Christ.

Tithing used to be a law. In the ancient days, priests of the Levitical Priesthood collected tithes from the Hebrew people who were, by law, required to pay up. The tithe paid constituted one-tenth of a person's income and could be a tenth of one's crop, a tenth of the number of sheep one owned, and so on.

While it is true that the ancient Hebrew days are gone, and with them the Levitical Priesthood (and other Priesthoods before that), God, nevertheless, requires that His ministry on earth be financed by the tithing system. But, whereas people who lived in Old Testament Israel were required by law to pay tithes for the purpose of helping the priests of those days to disseminate information about God, and so on, there is no law today that compels individuals to provide money for such purposes.

BASIS OF THE TITHING SYSTEM

Why, indeed, must you pay any money to God? Why does God want you to pay him part

YOU CAN TAKE IT WITH YOU

of your income, preferably one-tenth of it?

To ensure that God's Word is properly propagated throughout the world, to ensure that God's ultimate plan for humanity is carried out, God has always maintained a Priesthood. The priesthood has taken various forms over the centuries; for example, from the Mosaic era until the arrival of Jesus Christ the Priesthood of God was constituted from the tribe of Levi. The Levitical Priesthood, and the Melchisedec Priesthood that preceded it, collected tithes from the Hebrew people in the name of God. The priests required the tithes thus received, whether they were given in the form of money, livestock, foodstuffs, etc., to help meet their human needs for food, shelter, and so on, since they (the priests) were not engaged in any 'normal' work which would bring them incomes to live on.

In the same way, the priests of today, as well as other persons or organizations genuinely engaged in the propagation of the Gospel or in other aspects of God's Work, are entitled on God's express instructions) to receive funds for the purpose of helping them to finance the work they do in the name of God.

Today, it is very expensive to undertake the proper propagation of God's Word; it is costly, for example, to send out and maintain missionaries in remote parts of the world. It is expensive to maintain the priests and other persons who devote their lives to the preaching of the Word-of-God, to assisting the poor, the sick and the suffering in various parts of the world.

These servants of God, and usually members of their families as well, devote their time and energies to God's holy purpose rather than to earning a 'normal' income as you probably do. Please remember, however, that, like you they are human and have human needs that should be met. They need food, clothes, shelter and means of transportation, among other things, if they are to do God's Work properly. And they do require money to meet these and their other important needs; but who should supply this money? God insists that You and I should provide the money; He demands that each income -earning person pays Him part of their incomes—traditionally, one-tenth of every income. Such payments then, when made, should be used for God's Work on earth.

A FARMER'S SECRET OF SUCCESS

Matt M. is a dairy farmer in Queensland; Australia. Matt, who is in his early forties, has a large herd of dairy cattle. Farmers on similar dairy farms that adjoin Matt's own farm do not understand why Matt's cattle look so much healthier, why his cattle give out so much milk,

YOU CAN TAKE IT WITH YOU

why Matt is, as a consequence, so prosperous!

Envious farming colleagues have found, from private investigations, that Matt uses virtually the same types of feed, the same type of medication and generally uses the same techniques of dairy farming that they use. So why does Matt do so well? Why are his animals so very much more productive than their own animals?

Matt, of course, knows the answer. He knows why he is so successful. For every month, he sends money to a national Christian organization which is devoted to the Work of God in several ways. Matt calls such payments "Giving the Old Man His due". And that 'Old Man' - God - makes sure, in turn, that Matt succeeds in his farming business.

IS YOUR INCOME REALLY YOURS?

Is the income you earn really yours? Although you obviously believe that the money you earn, your income, is yours it is, in reality, not yours but God's! Now, doesn't that sound ridiculous? After all, it is you who earns the money; it is you who works for it; so why shouldn't it be yours and yours alone? That, admittedly, is logical reasoning. Nevertheless, it is true that your income is, in reality, not yours.

YOU CAN TAKE IT WITH YOU

Look at it this way:

Your income, and all the material things that your money can buy comes directly or indirectly from the earth, or from things that exist in or on the earth or otherwise depend on the earth. The food you buy with your money, the clothes you wear, the house you live in, the car you drive, the jewelery, et cetera,—everything—are all traceable, directly or indirectly, to the earth. And, mind you, you did not produce the earth.

Certainly you 'worked for' your income. Probably you leave your comfortable home to your workplace everyday, and maybe between the hours of nine in the morning and five in the afternoon of each day, five days a week, really work hard. But who created that energy, the thinking processes, which you apply in physical or mental action to earn that income? God. Who sustains that energy, those thinking processes? God! Who created the very air you breathe?

If you are a farmer, say an arable farmer, you probably plant seeds, cuttings or seedlings; you probably plough the land before sowing your seeds; you probably, in addition, irrigate the farm. Whatever you do, you certainly require some amount of water, and of sunshine, to ensure that your crops grow properly and

YOU CAN TAKE IT WITH YOU

provide you with a good harvest. You may want to ask yourself a few questions, such as: who created the process responsible for the seed's germination and subsequent growth? Who provides the water used for irrigation? Who, by the way, provided the soil in the first place? What about the rain? What about the sunshine the plant needs for its proper growth? God!

But maybe you are not a farmer, but say, a jeweler, earning your living by selling items of jewelery to other people. In that case, ask yourself where the minerals (gold, diamond, etc.) for making the jewellery you sell came from in the first instance? From the earth, of course, and it was God who created the earth, your very self, as well as many other things. If, on the other hand, you are neither a farmer nora jeweler but, let's suppose, a salesperson. What do you sell? Where does whatever you sell really come from?

Whatever the nature of your work, when you really consider it in this light, you find that God, in one way or another, is responsible, directly or indirectly, for its creation. God is also responsible for the supply of the physical and mental energies you require for the proper performance of your work, the work that brings you the income you live on.

Yes, you do take some initiative; you do

YOU CAN TAKE IT WITH YOU

plan, organise and co-ordinate resources, and so on. In totality, however, all this adds up to only an infinitesimal proportion of the final output or product of your work, whether such output is tangible or intangible. One would say that God supplies, directly or indirectly, about nine-tenths of everything, commodity or service, that man produces. Think hard about this and you will, hopefully, come to understand that your income is really not yours, that you do owe God some gratitude for all the assistance He gives you.

It is on this basis that God demands that YOU pay Him a small part of your income, traditionally a mere one-tenth of it (although you may give whatever amount you can afford), for the purpose of spreading His word, for the purpose of doing His work on earth for the ultimate benefit of mankind.

A SALESMAN DISCOVERS
THE MAGIC OF TITHING

When Stan K., a saleman who lives and works in the Canadian city of Montreal, first learned about the Magical Financial Law of Tithing from a close friend, he was sceptical. Regularly send out money to a church or some other organization genuinely engaged in the Work of

YOU CAN TAKE IT WITH YOU

God? Why should he do that?, Stan asked himself after he had learned about tithing. After all what has any church, or any other organization for that matter, done for him?

Stan worked very hard as a salesman for a local business establishment, moving from house to house in the attempt to sell a new household appliance to housewives. In a company where the bulk of a saleman's earnings depended on how much commission he made (which commission, in turn, depended on the volume of sales—the number of units sold—that he made), the going was frequently far from rosy for Stan.

Unfortunately for him, the sales territories allocated to Stan usually proved most unprofitable. Not that he didn't know how to sell properly; in fact, he could sweet-talk the average prospective customer into parting with their money, but the problem was that he often had to contend with very tough housewives, women who would stare at him so hard that he was relieved to leave their homes!

However, he made enough money to pay the rent and to support his wife and young daughter... nothing more. And now someone has the temerity to suggest that he regularly give part of his scant earnings away! Stan gave nothing away, and his fortunes stayed the

YOU CAN TAKE IT WITH YOU

same—poor.

In hindsight, subsequently, Stan noted that the friend who recommended tithing to him, an engineer by profession, was quite financially successful. Could there be some truth in what the man said? Stan wondered. Later on he went to see his friend, the engineer, about how to go about practicing tithing.

A few weeks after Stan began tithing on a regular basis he found that his commissions had soared because he was able to make more sales than previously. He noted that his sales territories were proving increasingly profitable; prospective buyers were nicer and more prepared to listen to him. Housewives, Stan noted, rather than slam the door in his face or insist on a free sample of the product he sold, were more prepared to listen and to buy from him.

Today, Stan is one of the most successful salesmen in the company. His commission has more than tripled and, in addition, his bosses have raised his basic pay!

WHY YOU SHOULD PAY GOD WHAT YOU OWE HIM

When you work for someone you do demand payment, don't you? When you expend your time and energy (which, as we have dis-

YOU CAN TAKE IT WITH YOU

cussed, aren't really yours, anyway) you demand to be paid for your trouble. Suppose your employer refused, unjustifiably, to pay you for the work you do. What would you do; shake his or her hand? Or give him a warm smile and a pat on the shoulder? No, you wouldn't! You would, instead, be angry; you may even seek redress in a court of law and justifiably so. But what do YOU pay God for all He does for you? What do you pay Him for the mental and physical energies he gives you, energies which enable you to work for a living? What do you pay Him for the air you breathe, for the lovely sunshine, and for the other good things you enjoy? What do you pay Him for the materials you use in your work—materials which, as we have noted, are part of God's creation? Let's face the fact: you, probably, don't pay a penny!

All that Jehovah, God, is saying is that YOU owe Him a proportion of your income. He is not demanding one-half of your earnings, not even one-fourth of it. All He wants is a mere one-tenth (or more or less, depending on your circumstances) of your earnings. Think about it. Think about all the assistance God gives you, assistance that enables you to work for a living.

Suppose that you were God. Then, knowing that you were directly or indirectly responsible for supplying about nine-tenths (or more)

YOU CAN TAKE IT WITH YOU

of the inputs (physical materials, mental and physical energies, what-have-you) needed for individual human output, you, probably, would ask not for a mere one-tenth of the reward—whether such reward is in terms of cash, livestock, foodstuffs, etc.—but for nine-tenths of it! That, I must say, would make good business sense; that would be fair, wouldn't it? But God asks for only a mere fraction of your income. He is entitled to a part of your income -i.e. by right!

Mind you, God is not begging you to give Him part of your income; neither is the Good Lord asking you to LEND him your money. Rather, He is DEMANDING that you PAY BACK what you owe Him and, let's face it, we, as individuals and as a group, owe Him a lot.

God's LAW reveals that when YOU regularly and honestly pay Him what you owe Him (i.e. part of your income) then HE, in turn, WILL ensure that you never want, financially, materially, etc. He promises that when you pay Him your debt, regularly and honestly, your financial and other needs will always be supplied by Him. The proof is in the Holy Bible, as well as in the rewarding experiences of several ordinary men and women.

At Proverbs, Chapter 3 verses 9-10 (New World Translation of the Holy Bible) it is writ-

YOU CAN TAKE IT WITH YOU

ten:

"Honour Jehovah with your valuable things and with the first fruits of all your produce.

"Then, your stores of supply will be filled with plenty; and with new wine your own press vats will overflow".

Pay up and see if the Lord won't ensure that your requirements are always met!

CHUKWU TITHES FOR PROGRESS

That Chukwuemeka O. had made very fast progress in the firm he worked for, a brewery, was undoubted. He had joined the brewery, based at Benin City in Nigeria, only a few years earlier, but he had been promoted several times, so many times that some of his colleagues had begun to wonder whether he had a special relationship with one or more of the company's top executives,

Chukwu had learnt about tithing soon after he left secondary school and had put it into practice ever since. Each month, whenever he received his pay packet, Chukwu would set aside one-tenth of it and divide this tenth further into four parts. Then, on every Sunday during the following month, Chukwu would go to church and donate a part of the money set aside for tithing. Although he earned only about N100

YOU CAN TAKE IT WITH YOU

a month, Chukwu never failed to tithe regularly.

He was surprised to note that the production manager, in whose department Chukwu worked, had suddenly taken a keen interest in him. The man had invited him for a discussion on two separate occasions and, during those discussions, had encouraged Chukwu to further his education through a correspondence course —a piece of advice which Chukwu promptly followed. On completion of the course, Chukwu notified his boss of his success and, not long after that, was promoted.

Although he never studied again he was, nevertheless, promoted several more times until he came to occupy quite a responsible position in the company—that of foreman.

While envious colleagues marvel at his "luck," Chukwu understands and knows the principal reason for his remarkable progress in the company—his regular and honest payment of his tithe.

HOW TO PRACTISE TITHING

1. Who Should you Give Your Tithes To? That depends entirely on you. You cannot, of course, personally hand over your lithe to God. Neither can you mail a cheque to God. So how do you pay your tithe?

YOU CAN TAKE IT WITH YOU

Since you cannot personally see God, let alone hand over your tithe to Him personally, He has instructed that you pay your tithe to Him through His earthly representatives—the church (any church) or other institution (genuinely) dedicated to the Work of God in any of several ways—such as preaching the Gospel, assisting the poor, the sick and the elderly, etc. Your payment may also be made personally to any genuine representative of God, such as a true minister of a church or a genuine official of a similar institution dedicated to the Work of God.

You may, for example, instruct your bank to send out some money from your bank account to an institution of your choice on a regular basis.

You can, if you are a regular churchgoer, decide, instead, to make donations to the church whenever you attend a church service.

The most important thing is to ensure that your money actually goes to a church of God or other institution genuinely committed to the Work of God.

2. How Much To Pay

Again, that depends entirely on you. It is not obligatory to give exactly one-tenth of your earnings for the work of God. You can give any amount, however small or large, depending on your circumstances. The important thing is to give honestly and of your own free will, not grudgingly.

Pay up willingly and happily in the sure knowledge that God will amply reward you for your efforts.

3. When Should You Pay Your Tithes?

You may pay weekly, monthly or even quarterly. Longer-term payments are usually inadvisable, though. Whichever you settle on, you should endeavour to pay your tithes regularly.

4. Can You Pay in Kind?

In today's modern world it is recognized that very few people can pay their tithes in livestock, foodstuffs, etc., as the Hebrews often used to do. However, you can regularly render, free of charge, service which, in one way or another, helps the Work of God. You may, of course, also give non-monetary tangible gifts to a church (or other similar institution engaged in the work of God) if that is feasible in the area you live.

5. Should You Tell Other People About Your Payments?

Certainly not! There is no need to attempt to show others what a do-gooder you are by telling anyone who cares to listen that you pay your tithe regularly. The important thing is that God,

YOU CAN TAKE IT WITH YOU

to whom payment is indirectly made, knows that you do pay your tithes regularly, and He will bless and reward you accordingly. It makes no difference, however, if your marriage partner finds out about your payments.

BEFORE PAYING YOUR TITHES

Before paying your tithe sit down, relax your body and mind by the breathing exercises described in the previous chapter and say the following aloud;

"I pay my tithes as thou commanded, O Jehovah. I know that you will send me your blessings."

Close your eyes again and see, in your mind, your money (or payment in other form), plus those of other people who have also paid their tithes, helping to do the Work of God. See, still in your mind, your money helping to propagate the Word of God in remote parts of the world; see your money helping to combat poverty, sickness, etc., around the world. See people having been made happier and healthier as a result of the assistance given by you and others. See, for example, ministers of God going joyously about their duties, their needs having been met partly because of the payments made by you and other people.

YOU CAN TAKE IT WITH YOU

Finally, see yourself, in your mind, as having achieved all your financial and other goals in life as a result of divine assistance.

THE MAN WHO MINDS THE CHURCH BELL

It is dawn in a tiny village in the American state of Arkansas. A middle-aged man is trudging towards the small church, his hands deeply thrust in the pockets of his overcoat, the collar of which is turned up against the bitterly cold wind.

The man soon reaches his destination and deftly pulls at a rope several times, sounding the bell that would awaken the Christian faithful to proceed to the church for the early morning worship.

Sid C., the man who minds the church bell, has been doing this voluntary service for over a decade. Sid says it is his way of "paying his bills to God" for all the wonderful things HE has done for him.

Sid is not wealthy, but he has all the money he will ever need for his poultry business which has grown from strength to strength over the years. His chickens are healthy, and his farm produces big, fresh eggs which find a ready market in the nearby larger towns.

YOU CAN TAKE IT WITH YOU

As Sidney walks back home after ringing the bell, he whistles happily to himself. He knows that he will come back at dawn the next day, and the day after that, and many, many more days subsequently, for as long as he lives. Sid loves doing something, however insignificant bell-ringing may seem to other people, in the service of God. For Sid knows, from personal experience, that that is a sure way to prosperity in all aspects of life.

WHAT HAPPENS WHEN YOU DON'T PAY UP?

God certainly isn't pleased with persons who refuse to pay Him their tithes. In fact He considers such refusal of payment as "robbery". This is made evident in the Bible. At Malachi 3: 8-10 of the Holy Bible (New World Translation) it is written:

"Will earthling man rob God? But you are robbing me". And you have said: "In what way have we robbed you?"

"In the tenth parts and in the contributions. With the curse you are cursing me, and ME you are robbing the nation in its entirety.

Bring all the tenth parts into the storehouse, that there may come to be food in my house, and test me out, please, in this respect," Jehovah of *armies has said, "whether I shall not open to YOU people the floodgates of the heavens and actually empty out upon YOU a blessing until there is no more want."*

From the foregoing we realize that:

1. God regards non-payment of tithes ("tenth parts") as robbery.

2. God promises that He will bless all people who regularly and honestly pay their tithes. He, Jehovah, will remove all want from the lives of all persons who add to the resources in his 'storehouse' by paying their tithes and thereby assisting, in their own small ways, the performance of His Work on earth. Those who refuse to pay up? Well, God doesn't like people who refuse to pay their debts they owe Him! And he withholds from such persons the blessings that should bring actual prosperity and happiness.

So: why don't YOU start paying NOW and start receiving the blessings God has promised??

IMPORTANT POINTS TO NOTE.

1. You will receive God's blessing when you make it to regularly, freely and joyously, pay part of your income out to aid the Work of God on earth. Not only will you, by doing this,

YOU CAN TAKE IT WITH YOU

receive financial blessings but blessings in other areas of your life.

2. You should send not necessarily exactly one-tenth of your income but any amount you can comfortably and honestly afford.

3. The income you earn is really not yours but God's. God is consequently entitled to a part of it.

4. Your payments should be made to individuals or institutions genuinely engaged in the work of God.

5. You may make your payments whenever you want; it is important, however, that you make them regularly.

6. You may pay in kind if that is feasible.

7. As much as is possible, keep your payments to yourself, without divulging to others that you pay tithes.

YOU CAN TAKE IT WITH YOU

Chapter Three
THE LAW OF MULTIPLE RETURNS
Quite similar to the Law of Tithing is the Law of Multiple Returns.

Definition: In simple terms, the Law of Multiple Returns (as it regards money) states that money given out to help other human beings who are genuinely suffering in one way or another will return to the sender several times over.

Almost all wealthy people, knowingly or unknowingly, apply this law. You may have noted that whenever there is a disaster of one kind or another—say, a terrible earthquake that kills, injures and renders several people homeless; floods; famine; a serious accident; etc.—any occurrence that brings hardship or suffering upon a large number of people—several

YOU CAN TAKE IT WITH YOU

other people rush to the aid of the surviving victims with cash and material donations to help alleviate their suffering.

Most of these donors, who usually (and I must say, wisely) prefer to remain anonymous, know that money spent in helping to alleviate the suffering of other human beings, provided such donation is made lovingly and willingly, is not money wasted but is money that will return to them (the donors) several times over.

It is a law that has worked time and time again for those who apply it. It is a law that will work for you as well, provided you apply it as recommended.

BASIS OF THE LAW OF MULTIPLE RETURNS

In the Holy Bible, Jesus Christ promises, at Luke 6:38 (New World Translation of the Bible), that those who give freely and lovingly will be given abundantly in return:

"Practice giving, and people will give to YOU. They will pour into YOUR laps a fine measure, pressed down, shaken together and overflowing.

"For with the measure that you are measuring out, they will measure out to YOU in return".

YOU CAN TAKE IT WITH YOU

Give freely and without hesitation and whatever you give out will return to you many times over. This is a law the Rich of this world know, keep to themselves, and exploit regularly.

HOW A MILLIONNAIRE INCREASES HIS WEALTH.

Gerald O. (that is not his real name) is considered as one of the fifty richest persons in America.

Gerald has, for as long as he can remember, applied this secret Law that his late father had revealed to him—the secret that money given out freely and joyously to ease the pain and suffering of other human beings will definitely come back into the possession of the giver, several times over.

Famine in some part of the Third World? Gerald sends off a cheque, through the appropriate channels, to help ease the hunger of those people involved. Refugees from Indonesia? Gerald sends some money to help alleviate their suffering. A devastating earthquake? Floods in Bangladesh? A maritime disaster? Gerry never fails to send something to aid the victims.

No wonder he is so successful financially! His businesses have continued to show good

YOU CAN TAKE IT WITH YOU

profit year after year, despite the recession, making Gerry a multi-millionaire.

He knows that for as long as he continues to give freely and happily to alleviate human suffering, his own personal finances cannot help but multiply.

HOW MUCH SHOULD YOU GIVE?

That depends on your current financial status. You can give whatever sum you can honesttly afford. But, admittedly, the more you give the more you will receive in return.

The most important thing to note is that you must give your donation freely and happily, in the sure knowledge that the amount you give will return to you many times over.

Decide on how much you can comfortably afford to give away, then send the amount away to help alleviate the pain and suffering of other human beings.

Please note that you may send different sums of money at various times, depending on your financial circumstances and on the nature of the problems that you want to help solve.

YOU CAN TAKE IT WITH YOU

WHO SHOULD YOU GIVE YOUR DONATION TO?

a) Your donation may be given to any group of people (whether in your own country or elsewhere in the world) who are genuinely in need of financial or other material assistance to help them to tide over difficult conditions. These people may be surviving victims of natural disasters such as floods, earthquakes, droughts, volcanic eruptions, etc, or man-made ones such as wars.

Whatever the situations, please make sure that you send your money through the proper channels, such as organizations genuinely committed to relieving the hardships of the persons involved in the particular disaster.

(b) Money may also be sent to organizations or institutions working to find antidotes to some of mankind's problems; organizations engaged in research geared to finding cures for common or particularly dangerous diseases, for example, may be chosen as the direct recipients of your donation. Such organizations frequently advertise their cases in the quality papers, and they provide addresses to which donations may be sent.

By giving to such organizations you help their work to find solutions to some of the prob-

YOU CAN TAKE IT WITH YOU

lems facing other human beings; you help reduce pain and unhappiness. And you will be amply rewarded.

Finally, you may give directly to any particular individual who is in dire need of financial or other assistance. For example, if you are a housewife, you may frequently (especially during the bitterly cold winter months) send a bowl of soup to that lonely elderly lady who lives next door and who, from all indications, requires human company as well as material assistance of one type or another.

By all means give something out to help a fellow human being in need, for not only does doing that make you feel good but, in addition, it will bring you ample material (financial) rewards in the future.

HOW THE LAW OF MULTIPLE RETURNS HELPED BAYO

Bayo D. had learned about the Law of Multiple Returns and its application a few months earlier from a friend but had never got down to applying it. Unknown to Bayo, a college student of Lagos, Nigeria, however, he was soon to have an opportunity to apply the Law.

Bayo was returning home from college one hot afternoon, after classes. Bayo was on a

YOU CAN TAKE IT WITH YOU

taxi alone; a few minutes later, a well-dressed man signalled the taxi driver to stop the car and, when the driver did so, got in the taxi after the driver had assured him he was going his (the man's) way.

The taxi stopped a short distance from Bayo's destination for the man to get off. Before he got off, the man felt his back trouser pocket for his wallet, meaning to get money from it to pay the N3 fare the taxi driver had charged. But the wallet was gone! The man told the driver about his predicament but the driver was unconvinced. The burly driver got out of the car, pulled the man out of the taxi, grabbed the collar of his shirt and shook him ferociously, shouting: "Pay up! I've seen your type before!! You get in a taxi and expect to get a free ride! Well, not in my taxi!" A small crowd was already beginning to form and a few school kids were jeering loudly: "Pay the man! Give him his money!" The man, almost sobbing, was loudly explaining that a pick-pocket must have stolen his wallet for he was sure he had it only a few hours earlier. He turned and looked at Bayo, his eyes pleading for help.

Bayo sized up the situation. Lagos!, he said to himself. Was the man telling the truth? Was he? Bayo was well aware that there were so many crooks on the streets of Lagos (as in any

YOU CAN TAKE IT WITH YOU

other major city) that one was often not certain who was really trustworthy. Was this man a crook or an honest man who was genuinely in unanticipated diffculty? Bayo wondered. Meanwhile the taxi drver, then very excited, was pushing the man around; the school kids were jeering more loudly and the crowd was getting bigger. Making up his mind, Bayo got out of the taxi, removed N3 from his wallet and gave it to the man who paid the driver. The crowd began to disperse, some of the people obviously disappointed at having been denied the chance to watch a fight for free.

The man wanted to collect Bayo's address, explaining that he would repay the amount later that day. But Bayo refused, and the taxi later took him to his destination.

Two days later, Bayo found a $20 note in the street when out shopping with his sister. The very next day he found a $10 note, again in the streets. Since nobody around seemed to have dropped either the $20or the $10 note, Bayo pocketed them. Was his finding the currency notes mere coincidences or did it have something to do with the help he gave the man a few days earlier?, Bayo wondered. About a week later, a friend who owed him some money and had refused to repay him suddenly paid back the money: $25.

YOU CAN TAKE IT WITH YOU

Bayo is now convinced that the Law of Multiple Return does work; he never fails to give some help, financially or otherwise, to other human beings who, in his opinion, are in genuine need of assistance. Is it surprising that he has continued to achieve success after success in all facets of his life?

WHEN SHOULD YOU GIVE YOUR DONATION/ASSISTANCE?

Give your donation (or other assistance) whenever the occasion demands. For example, when you learn about a disaster of one kind or another, find out where donations may be sent. Frequently, funds are set up and appropiate addresses are given (usually on television, during news broadcasts) to which donations may be sent. PLEASE SEND SOMETHING, even if it is only a £1 $1 or Ll ! Send it freely, joyously and without hesitation, confident that the money you send will come back to you many times over.

Furthermore, do not give once only. Make it a habit to contribute as much or as little as you can afford whenever the occasion arises.

YOU CAN TAKE IT WITH YOU

HOW WILL THE MONEY YOU GIVE OUT COME BACK TO YOU?

Frankly, I don't know how the money you donate for the assistance of other people will come back to you. It may come back (several multiples of it, that is) in any of several ways.

For example, if you are engaged in your own private business your profits could increase steadily and tremendously; you may find that you attract many more customers, some of whom may be big-spenders.

If, on the other hand, you are a working person, you may get a raise from your employer, probably a bigger raise than you ever anticipated, and, maybe, more frequently, too.

Then, if you are a betting person you may frequently win big prizes that more than compensate for the donations you had made. You may even stumble upon some missing money which nobody subsequently claims. A close relative or friend may, unexpectedly, leave you money in a will.

The important thing to know is that your money will come back, multiplied several times over, to you provided you give it away freely, happily and without hesitation.

YOU CAN TAKE IT WITH YOU

CAN YOU GIVE IN KIND?

Yes, you can. For example, if the persons you wish to assist are flood victims, you may send some blankets. What you give will, of course, depend on the nature of the particular problem.

WHAT TO DO BEFORE YOU GIVE AWAY YOUR MONEY

Before you part with your money, or before you render any particular assistance that is calculated to aid suffering people or a suffering person, please do either of the following:

(a) If you have the time, sit down and relax your body and mind as has been described in Chapter One. In your mind, imagine that you see people to whom the donation is meant to go or for whose benefit your money will be given. Imagine them in their current difficult conditions; then see them, in your mind, benefitting by your donation and donations sent by other people. In your mind, see them in better conditions, happier circumstances. It is helpful if you are holding the cheque or cash you wish to send in your hand as you form these mental images. Your eyes should be closed as you form the mental images. Finally, say the following (once only):

YOU CAN TAKE IT WITH YOU

"I send the sum of (state the amount) to mention who the ultimate beneficiaries of your donation are/is) to help enable them/him/her (delete as appropriate overcome (state the nature of the problem). I believe that this sum will return to me many times over. I believe that it will bring blessings to me and to those to whom I send it."

Then imagine that your own financial goals have been met, that your donation has brought many blessings upon you.

After this, open your eyes and send the money. If your donation is in kind, follow the same procedure, substituting the appropriate words for "the sum of," etc, in the above statement as necessary.

(b) If there is no time for you to sit down to do as has been suggested above, such as the situation in the case of Bayo (in the story mentioned elsewhere above) then all you have to do, before parting with your money or rendering assistance in another way, is to make a quick mental note of that fact. In your mind, quickly but firmly say the following (once only): "I give/ render this service (say what or how much, as appropriate) to help (state who) overcome (state nature of problem). I believe that I will receive, in return many blessings for my assistance. I believe that this sum service (state) will

YOU CAN TAKE IT WITH YOU

come back to me several times over"

Please note that you do not have to repeat what has been stated above word-for-word. Instead, you may use your own words that mean the same thing.

WHY DOES THIS LAW WORK?

As previously mentioned, the basis of this Law is mystical. Jesus himself asserted that whoever gives (freely and joyously) in the service of others will be given in return.

Apart from this mystical guarantee to the one who gives freely and lovingly, it is probable lhat the prayers (silent or vocal) of the beneficiaries of your donation or other assistance brings blessings upon you and other donors.

IMPORTANT POINTS TO NOTE

1. If you give freely, joyously and lovingly to help people in difficulty, you will be given abundantly in return—financially, materially and in many other ways.

2. You may give any sum of money you can comfortably afford. You may also give in kind when the occasion demands that you do so.

3. You may send your donation through organisations or institutions who are genuinely

YOU CAN TAKE IT WITH YOU

working to alleviate the suffering of the group of persons concerned. You may, however, give directly to individuals who, in your opinion, are genuinely in need of your assistance.

4. The Returns may come to you in any one or more of several ways.

5. Before you give away your money, or before you render some useful assistance to a person or a group of people in need, mentally acknowledge that you are going to do so and that you know that you will receive blessings accordingly.

YOU CAN TAKE IT WITH YOU

Chapter Four
THE LAW OF INCREASE
Definition:

The Law of Increase states that if you habitually wish for increase (i.e. abundance of wealth, of good health, of peace and general happiness, etc.) for other people you come into contact with, you ultimately attract these very things into your own life.

The converse of this Law also holds true.

In a previous chapter, you have been shown how you can improve your financial status by habitually focussing your mind on wealth and the good things wealth can bring.

While it is very important, as emphasized at length in the first chapter of this book, that you develop the habit of regularly and persis-

YOU CAN TAKE IT WITH YOU

tently focussing your mind on wealth for yourself, it is equally important that you are made aware of the fact that your thoughts about other people, particularly those you come into personal contact with during your day-to-day activities, do affect your own personal fortunes in life!

THOUGHTS HAVE WINGS!

Your thoughts have wings! Other people are able to, subconsciously, sense what you think about them; other people can sense whether you like or despise them, however well you attempt to conceal the fact through pretence.

How other people will relate to you will depend greatly on what they think you think of them. If they had sensed that you like them, that you think of them with love and kindness, that you wish them progress and happiness in all facets of their lives, then they cannot help but react or respond positively to you. They will be prepared, then, to throw in their lot with you; they will be prepared to assist you, as best as they can to help you to attain your financial and other goals in life.

But what happens when other people sense that you dislike them? That you do not

YOU CAN TAKE IT WITH YOU

wish them well? They will, as best as they can, avoid your company; they will be most reluctant to assist you to attain your goals in life. They may even attempt to, directly or indirectly, sabotage your efforts at personal progress!

How important it is, therefore, that you think about other people with love! How useful it is to bless other people, to wish for them increase (i.e., abundance) in all aspects of their lives, for by doing so you attract those very things into your own dear life!

YOU NEED OTHER PEOPLE'S HELP TO BECOME RICH!

Whatever the nature of your present occupation or profession, whatever your present financial standing, you certainly need the help of other people to achieve greater financial progress.

In your occupation, you require the support, the assistance of other people—colleagues, subordinates, superiors—if you are to make progress. If you are, for example, frequently at loggerheads with your superiors it is possible that you will not achieve any quick advancement, if at all. Similarly, if your colleagues or subordinates dislike you they could make things very uncomfortable for you.

YOU CAN TAKE IT WITH YOU

If other people work for you then it is even more important that you endeavour to be on good terms with your employees, that you make the effort to like them as fellows human beings. This, of course, does not mean that you must tolerate laziness and other bad habits in your employees. Rather, while it is necessary to be fair but firm with them by meting out punishment when such punishment is necessary, it is imperative that you make a deliberate effort to be interested in them, to love them as human beings.

It is only when they sense that you like them, that you wish them well, that you have their welfare (as individuals and as a group) at heart, that they will wholeheartedly work for the organizational good and, consequently, for your personal financial prosperity.

So, you see, it is essential that you make a deliberate, honest effort to like other people, to wish them well, to wish for them the good things of life, just as you wish these very things for yourself.

And you start in your mind!

YOU CAN TAKE IT WITH YOU
WHY JANE IS SO POPULAR AND PROGRESSIVE

Jane S., aged twenty-two years and working as a typist in a business establishment at Newcastle-upon-Tyne, in the north of England, is easily the most popular and fast progressing woman in the department. Some of her colleagues are, of course, envious of her—envious of the fact that Jane is well liked by all the senior officers as well as by many of her own colleagues at the typing pool. She has recently been promoted over the heads of some of her longer-serving colleagues. But what is Jane's secret of success?

Several times each week, Jane sits down, at home and in her favourite armchair, relaxes her body and mind, and sends thoughts of love to several of the individuals she works with. One day she may concentrate on her superiors; another day she will focus thoughts of love on her colleagues, moving from one individual to another. She does the same for members of her family and other persons she knows.

In her mind, Jane clearly pictures the person she is concentrating on at the particular time; still in her mind, Jane talks to this person, telling him (or her) that she likes him, that she wishes him prosperity in all areas of his life. In her mind, she sees the person nodding his head

YOU CAN TAKE IT WITH YOU

in agreement; she hears the person saying he likes her too. Jane focuses her mind, throughout each week and during her spare time, on every individual in her (small) department until everyone, superior or colleague, has been considered.

In real life, the others don't understand why they are so attracted to Jane; they wonder why they like her so much.

Jane, of course, knows why.

WHEN SHOULD YOU APPLY THE LAW OF INCREASE?

Put the Law into application whenever you can. As often as you can manage, relax and send thoughts of love, thoughts of kindness, to some other person you know. See, in your mind, this person improving financially and in several other ways. Speak to the person, in your mind, telling him or her about your love for them, about your desire that they prosper in all facets of life. Do this time and again, and from person to person; ultimately the people concerned cannot help but be drawn to you; they cannot help but become more friendly with you and to assist you, as best as they can, to achieve your own financial and other objectives.

YOU CAN TAKE IT WITH YOU

WHICH PEOPLE TO CONSIDER WHEN APPLYING THE LAW

It is preferable that you commence with the people around you in your daily life: members of your family, colleagues at work, other friends, and so on.

Move from one individual to another, sending them thoughts of love and prosperity; they will receive these thoughts—be assured of that fact—and by the universal law of attraction, will become closer to you, will like you in return, and will do the best that they can to assist you.

HOW TO APPLY THE LAW

You may, if you wish, focus your mind on thoughts of love and prosperity for other persons immediately after you have concentrated on wealth, etc., for yourself as described in Chapter One. You may, alternatively, set aside a different time for concentrating on prosperity for others.

Having decided on the time, this, then is what you should do:

(a) Relax completely the way you have been taught in Chapter One.

(b) After letting your mind dwell awhile

YOU CAN TAKE IT WITH YOU

on the scenic view of the lake (please refer to chapter one), imagine that you see the person you wish to influence very clearly. In your mind, see the person's face clearly; see him (or her) standing or sitting facing you, then, still in your mind, see that you and the person are looking at each other, eye to eye.

(c) In your mind, hear yourself talking to the person. Hear yourself tell the person that you like him (or her), that you wish him well, that you wish him financial prosperity as well as the other good things of life. See and hear him agreeing with you. Hear him say he likes you as well; hear him say that he will, henceforth, behave nicely towards you, act in your favour, and so on.

(d) If you have any specific requests, any particular favour you wish the person in question to do for you, tell him (in your mind) about it. Then hear him, still in your mind, agreeing to do as you wish. Ask this favour of him on several occasions (and on each occasion, see and hear him agree to do your wish) before asking the favour in real life.

(e) From this individual, move on to another person, going through the entire procedure described above.

You will notice, after regularly and diligently carrying out the suggestions above for

YOU CAN TAKE IT WITH YOU

some time, that the people around you in your day-to-day life are more willing to co-operate with you, are kinder and more understanding, are more willing to assist you to achieve your objections.

WHY RICK'S EMPLOYEES ARE SO PRODUCTIVE

Rick N., aged forty-seven years, owns and runs a small advertising agency in Los Angeles, USA. Today Rick's business is doing very well, making bigger profits year after year. But things had not always been so good for Rick.

Long-standing employees would tell you that Rick used to be one of the most cantankerous, most self-centred, most arrogant men they had ever come across! Some would add that he was a most inhumane individual!! He was even often very reluctant to allow employees who were obviously ill to take some days off from work. In short, Rick believed in driving his employees and in treating them as mere 'cogs in the wheel'. Naturally, his employees resented him. Naturally, his employees worked hard only when he was looking; they did things their own way whenever his back was turned.

Consequently, productivity was low, work was done haphazardly, and fewer clients came

YOU CAN TAKE IT WITH YOU

back to his company. Profits, therefore, were very small if at all there was any. Employees quit very often.

Then Rick learned about the Law of Increase. He learned that by regularly sending his employees thoughts of love, kindness and prosperity, he would, in return, win their love and goodwill; that he would win their cooperation in the interest of the company.

Every morning after Rick learned about the Law, before he left home for work, he would sit down, relax and for about thirty minutes focus his mind on thoughts of love, kindness and prosperity for each member of his staff. In his mind, he talked to each of them, asking for their individual and collective cooperation. He let them understand that, deep down, he loved them, that he wished them well.

The positive results came after only a week. Rick noticed that employees, who generally avoided him unless it was essential that they meet him to discuss an aspect of the company's business, had begun to warm up to him. Rick did his best to encourage this new relationship and very soon he realized changes in other areas as well. He noted that employees worked harder, were willing to stay longer at work when the situation demanded and were very productive. Clients noticed the change,

YOU CAN TAKE IT WITH YOU

too, and came back again and again, recommending Rick's establishment to their friends. Rick's business boomed, and his profits soared.

Today Rick has a fantastic relationship with his employees. He still sends them thoughts of love, kindness and prosperity. And he still, as a consequence, receives their love, kindness and cooperation. They, the employees, still help Rick to make much more money than he ever thought possible.

A SIMPLE EXPERIMENT

Is there someone who, you are aware, dislikes you? Someone who wouldn't, for example, speak to you let alone cooperate with you? Someone you wish to have as a friend? If there is such a bothersome person then you may, if you wish, change him or her by the method described above. That is, after relaxing in the suggested manner, send thoughts of love, kindness and understanding to him. In your mind ask him for his cooperation, for his love and support, for his understanding. Wish him well; picture him as succeeding.

Do this about twice a day for about one week or more; then watch how this person subsequently reacts to you!

YOU CAN TAKE IT WITH YOU

WHY IS IT NECESSARY TO WISH FOR INCREASE FOR OTHER PEOPLE AS WELL AS FOR YOURSELF?

It is true that by imagining yourself, regularly and persistently, as financially prosperous, healthy, happy, etc., you do attract these very conditions into your life. The converse, of course, is also true.

Again, it is true that by picturing other people as prosperous, as happy, as cooperative, as kind, etc., you help attract those conditions into their lives. It is also a fact that by regularly imagining trouble, poverty, unhappiness, etc., for other people you actually help to bring those conditions into the lives of those people. You see, your mind is that powerful!

What happens when you habitually focus your mind on wealth, good health and other aspects of abundance (or "increase") for yourself but, concentrate your mind on imagining for other people poverty, misery, unhappiness, ill-health and other such conditions?

When that happens your subconscious mind receives (from you) conflicting "instructions". There you are, on the one hand, instructing your mind, through processes such as mental imagery or visualization, positve affirmations, etc., to bring you financial prosperity and other forms of increase while, simultaneously, you are "instructing" it to send the very opposite conditions into the lives of other people! These conflicting "instructions" may cancel themselves out, thus making it impossible for you to receive the good things you imagined for your own sweet self. On the other hand, if you had imagined (negatively) hard enough concerning the other person (or persons) you could attract into your own life those very negative conditions you wished for others!!

In view of this fact you must form the habit of focusing your mind on thoughts of wealth for yourself but, while doing so, do NOT dwell on thoughts of poverty, misery and unhappiness for other people!

DAILY AFFIRMATION

To help you benefit from the great power of the Law of Increase, repeat the following to yourself on a daily basis:

"I attract unto myself, by the power of God and by the power of my own mind, financial prosperity, good health and happiness in all aspects of my life. I attract God's blessings into my life. I know that my wishes will come true.

"I wish for other people financial prosperity, good health and all-round happiness in the same way that I wish these very things for myself.

"I ask for God's blessings for other people. I know that by wishing for other people prosperity and happiness, I wish these conditions for myself.

"I wish for prosperity and happiness not only for myself but for members of my family, for my colleagues at work, for my neighbour, for my friends, relatives and acquaintances as well as for my enemies and others who disagree with me. I wish for peace and understanding between myself and all other human beings.

"I wish for peace and understanding among the nations of the world, and amongst their peoples.

"I know that God will bring these wishes into reality".

IMPORTANT POINTS TO NOTE

1. You ultimately attract into your own life the very conditions you habitually wish for other people.

2. Form the habit of wishing for other people financial prosperity, good health and all-round happiness for, by doing so, you help to attract those conditions into your life as well as others.

YOU CAN TAKE IT WITH YOU

3. Your thoughts have wings! Other people will ultimately sense what you really think about them. The way other people relate to you will depend greatly on what they think you think of them.

4. To achieve (great) financial prosperity you need the help, the cooperation and support of other people.

5. Whether other people will support you, or freely co-operate with you, in your quest for financial and material success will greatly depend on your personal relationship with them.

Generally, they will lend you their support, their cooperation, only when they sense or know that you think well of them, that you wish for them prosperity and happiness.

6. By regularly affirming, preferably on a daily basis, that you acknowledge the importance of wishing for other people as well as for yourself the good things of life, it becomes easier for you to regularly apply the Law of Increase.

Chapter Five
THE LAW OF BELIEF
Definition

The Law of Belief (or of Faith) simply states that when you strongly believe that you possess the ability to attract financial and other riches—or, indeed, any other thing or condition for that matter—into your life, when you hold on to this belief or faith persistently you are ultimately propelled or galvanized into taking various measures which will bring you the financial and other riches you seek.

There is great power in Faith or Belief. Jesus Christ Himself underlined this fact when He said, at Mark 9:23 (in the Holy Bible), *"If thou cans't believe, all things are possible to him that believeth."*

Belief in oneself is an important quality which must be developed by anyone who wants to attain to a position of financial wealth and prosperity.

YOU CAN TAKE IT WITH YOU
NO VENTURE NO GAIN!

. . . . so the saying goes; and how very true! In our Western, capitalist societies there are numerous opportunities for anyone with the courage and enterprise to, through honest and legitimate means, achieve financial success.

The problem with most people is that they are too scared (probably of failure!) to seize any of the numerous opportunities that pass them by—opportunities which, had they been seized, could have brought them all the money they had ever wanted!

MIKE'S FINANCIAL SUCCESS

Mike F., aged thirty-two from Boston, Massachussetts, U. S.A, has long discarded the battered Volkswagon Beetle that he used to own and drive. Instead, Mike now drives a Caddy around his home-town, Boston. In addition, Mike no longer wears the faded blue jeans, the outworn sneakers and the leather jacket that almost always constituted parts of his entire clothing at any particular point in time. Today, he wears fashionable suits purchased from his city's most exclusive shops. And the girls no longer laugh at him; they no longer avoid his company as they did five years ago. Mike is still unmarried and intends to 'live it up' a few more years before

YOU CAN TAKE IT WITH YOU

committing himself to one woman.

Five years ago Mike sat down and took a good look at himself; he didn't like what he saw. Then aged twenty-eight, he realized that gradually he was wasting his life; he came to the decision that unless he took drastic measures his unenviable existence would continue for ever. Yes, he must do something positive about his humdrum life, and he should start immediately. For a beginning, he would think about how to make a lot more money than he currently did as a freelance photographer. He was sure that he was capable of making much more money if he explored the various business opportunities (which had frequently occurred to him in the past but which he had done nothing about) properly. Mike was certain that he could make much more money with his camera if he tried hard enough.

This is what Mike did:

1. He made up his mind that he should be in business within the next fortnight. Telephoning his parents, who had moved to live in California, Mike was able to convince them to lend him some money by post. In addition, he talked a close friend into giving him more money as a loan. With the sum thus obtained, Mike bought a bigger, better-quality camera.

2. With the little money he had in the bank,

YOU CAN TAKE IT WITH YOU

plus what he obtained by selling off his original camera, Mike bought several photographic films, packed a bag, and embarked on the first phase of his business plan. His plan involved the following:

(a) With his camera and the necessary photographic materials he travelled to popular holiday resorts and, without being asked to do so, took photographs of several of the holiday makers from vantage positions. It was a gamble, but several of the people agreed, later, to pay for the prints when they were contacted. They paid so well that Mike extended the service to nearby holiday resorts. As the pictures were good, the holiday makers usually accepted them. Besides, several holidaying families actually invited him to take photographs of them swimming, sailing, fishing, etc.

Some asked for enlargements of the prints and others paid for supplementary prints to be mailed to them at their homes. People on holiday, it seemed, were prepared to pay well for extra good photographs that would subsequently remind them of the happy times they had while on holiday.

(b) With permission, Mike took photographs of beautiful scenery around the holiday resorts and got these made into picture postcards. Copies of these were displayed in lob-

YOU CAN TAKE IT WITH YOU

bies of the hotels at the various holiday resorts. Mike was pleasantly surprised at the rate at which they were bought. He got more and more copies made to meet the demand.

(c) As often as he could, Mike took his camera to weddings, especially the big ones, and, without being asked to do so, would take photographs of the bride and bridegroom from several vantage positions. The prints actually told, at a glance, the story of each wedding, depicting several stages of the entire wedding that often escape other photographers. Mike mounts the prints in several attractive albums and sells them to the couple at a high price. The prints are invariably so good that no bride worth the name would refuse to purchase such remarkable reminders of easily the greatest day in her life.

(d) Finally, Mike commenced taking photographs from uncommon and vantage positions of important buildings and monuments in several cities and getting them turned into picture postcards which sold very well.

A few weeks after embarking on his business Mike found that he could not, single-handedly, cope with the great volume of business that came his way. Consequently, he hired local help whenever it was necessary to do so.

Five years have passed since Mike first

YOU CAN TAKE IT WITH YOU

had the courage to embark on his business venture. Today, he is rich. He doesn't have to work, for he has trained assistants who carry out most of his work for him.

FAITH IN YOURSELF

Virtually all the people who worked hard to make fortunes for themselves began from small beginnings. They had good business ideas (and, mind you, everyone gets a good business idea once in a while) which they had the guts, the courage or daring, to put into actual practice.

There usually was the risk of failure, but these people were not deterred; they plodded on tirelessly and courageously. These people believed that if others had succeeded financially, there was no earthly reason why they shouldn't succeed as well! They had faith in themselves, belief in their own capabilities. They usually had to borrow money from banks, friends, relatives, etc., to help them in their business ventures, but they were not afraid to be temporarily in debt.

They took business advice from knowledgeable persons, governmental advisory bodies and other institutions. Ultimately, they made it financially. They made more money

YOU CAN TAKE IT WITH YOU

than they ever thought possible. They were able, as a result of their much healthier financial circumstances, to buy and enjoy the use of virtually all the good things of life—expensive clothes and cars, luxurious houses, long holidays in the sun, sumptuous meals at plush restaurants; you know, those things which make you realize that life is, indeed, worth living; those things which usually tell the difference between rich and poor people!

WHAT TO DO

1. Convince yourself that people who have been able to succeed financially are, basically, not much different from you. You may, indeed, be more intelligent or better educated than several of them! What, probably, is the major difference between such people and yourself is the daring to actually put a business idea (or ideas) into practice. You, apparently, lack the courage to do so.

Even if another person who has made it financially inherited all his or her money or a great proportion of it, the fact still remains that a parent, grandparent or some forebear ancestor of his had the guts to begin from somewhere, had the courage to put a business idea into actual practice.

YOU CAN TAKE IT WITH YOU

Furthermore, please note that if someone in your work place receives a bigger pay than you do it may stem from the fact that he/she works harder or had the courage and foresight to undertake useful further studies, maybe through correspondence while still working.

2. Sit down and have a good look at your own life. Couldn't you really do with much more money? Of course, you could! Think of all the good things that extra money will enable you to do.

Then, take concrete steps to put a business idea into action. There are, for example, several home-run businesses which you can commence and run on a part-time basis, switching to full-time when the financial returns justify your doing so.

Several of such business opportunities are frequently advertised in the Classified Advertisements columns of local and national newspapers and magazines, etc.

3. Take positive steps to learn more about the various measures you can take to improve all facets of your life—financially and otherwise. You'll agree, I am sure, that to achieve all-round happiness in life you need more than a permanently fat bank account. That is why you need to read books that will enlighten you on the measures to take to achieve success in love, health,

YOU CAN TAKE IT WITH YOU

general interpersonal relationships, and so on.

IMPORTANT POINTS TO NOTE

1. Believe that you CAN become rich, that you possess the ability to attract financial and other riches into your life.

2. Your future is in your own hands! YOU are the architect of your own destiny!! Therefore, please do take immediate concrete steps to improve your life as herein suggested.

3. Make it a habit to be on the look-out for business opportunities that could successfully launch you on the road to financial prosperity. Workable business ideas, when received or discovered, should not be allowed to lie unutilised. Rather, put them into action NOW!

4. Frequently, you should endeavour to read books that will help to improve not only your financial status but also help you to achieve success in love, health, your general interpersonal relationships, etc. To this end, J must repeat that it will be most beneficial to you to write to **Timothy Green Beckley, Post Office Box 753, New Brunswick, New Jersey 08903**. He publishes a number of useful books which should help you achieve your goals in life.

GOOD LUCK!

YOU CAN TAKE IT WITH YOU

SPELLCRAFT, WISECRAFT, OCCULT, METAPHYSICAL WORKBOOKS AND STUDY GUIDES

Order From Amazon.com or direct from the publisher Timothy G Beckley Box 753, New Brunswick, NJ 08903

mrufo8@hotmail.com

Books By Maria D'Andrea

HEAVEN SENT MONEY SPELLS
IMAGINE RECEIVING MONEY JUST BY USING THE POWERS OF YOUR MIND! Let Maria D' Andrea Tell You How To Turn Your Dreams Into Cash — And Become A Virtual Human MONEY MAGNET. Inspired by the Heavenly Light. Here are spells that anyone can learn to execute. Use herbs, candles and gemstones to create prosperity! Have talismans and amulets help do the work for you!
   8.5x11—Workbook format—132 pages—ISBN-13: 978-1606111000—$19.95

SECRET OCCULT GALLERY AND SPELL CASTING FORMULARY
COME UP TO THE "GOOD LIFE" with Maria's top dozen enchantments and occult gallery of mystical and spiritual essentials. Easy to perform spells that could put you on easy street.
   8.5x11—Workbook format—152 pages—ISBN-13: 978-1606111284—$21.95

YOUR PERSONAL MEGA POWER SPELLS
A valuable interpretation of blessings, protections, hex-breaking rituals and ceremonies as practiced by the most ardent of Wiccans, alchemists, sages and occultists down through the centuries.
   8.5X11—252 pages—ISBN-13: 978-1606111055—$21.95

SECRET MAGICAL ELIXIRS OF LIFE
Explore The Paranormal Vibrations Of Crystals, Gems And Stones For Good Health, Enhanced Psychic Powers And Phenomenal Inner Strength!
   8.5X11—150 PAGES—ISBN-13: 978-1606111147—$21.95

YOU CAN TAKE IT WITH YOU

HOW TO ELIMINATE ANXIETY AND STRESS THROUGH THE OCCULT
Just utilize Crystals, Gemstones, Meditation, Herbs, Oils, Visualization, Chakras, Music, Prayer, Mandalas, Mantras, Incense, Candles and More.
6x9—150 pages—ISBN-13: 978-1606111383—$19.95

MYSTICAL, MAGICKAL BEASTS AND BEINGS
Come explore the supernatural side of man's best – and worst – "friends" as related in the strangest stories involving beasties of all sorts – seen and unseen. And uppermost learn how to get them to assist in our lives in a positive way. Other contributors include Penny Melis and Sean Casteel.
8.5x11—224 pages—ISBN-13: 978-1606111567—$21.95

OCCULT GRIMORIE AND MAGICAL FORMULARY
10 BOOKS ROLLED INTO ONE! – OVER 500 SPELLS! Reveals the secret of the ages. Manifest your destiny NOW! Most powerful spellcasters deliberately leave out important information. NOT MARIA!
8.5x11—236 pages—ISBN-13: 978-1606111086—$24.00

Books By William Oribello

THE MASTERBOOK OF SPIRITUAL POWER—The spells in this sacred text work like a magnet to attract big money, good health, love, freedom from tension and worry...as well as banishing curses and eroding negativity.
8.5x11—116 pages—ISBN-13: 978-1606111109—$18.95

THE SEALED MAGICAL BOOK OF MOSES—Here are arcane secrets of Moses' powers that can now be revealed to series students only. Includes the 21 MAGICAL TALISMANS OF MOSES seldom seen, which can give you the powers of the holy sage.
8.5x11—142 pages—ISBN-13: 978-0938294689—$18.95

CANDLE BURNING MAGIC WITH THE PSALMS—Create life's greatest blessings by combining the power of the Holy Psalms with the magic of burning different colored candles. Best times, days and conditions for spells.
8.5x11—188 pages—ISBN-13: 978-0938294580—$21.95

USING CANDLE BURNING TO CONTACT YOUR GUARDIAN ANGEL
8.5X11—100 pages—ISBN-13: 978-0938294757—$19.95

SACRED MAGIC REVISED—Forbidden knowledge now revealed...prosperity for all guaranteed! Includes seven great money secrets.
8.5x11—146 pages—ISBN-13: 978-1606111291—$18.95

YOU CAN TAKE IT WITH YOU

DIVINE BIBLE SPELLS—This book proves what you've heard all along – With God All Things Are Possible! Added material from Dragonstar.
8.5x11—142 pages—ISBN-13: 978-1606111499—$18.95

DIVINE MONEY SPELLS—Easy Magickal Spells To Jump Start Your Spiritual Economic Stimulus Package Added material from Dragonstar. Spells to eliminate poverty and to draw abundance.
8.5x11—152 pages—ISBN-13: 978-1606110645—$21.95

THE MEDIUMSHIP OF SPIRIT—The Ascension of William Alexander Oribello. Now an Ascended Master, Oribello has returned to the Earth Plane to continue his great work, assisted by the mediumship of psychic Aurora Thyme...
8.5X11—122 pages—ISBN-13: 978-1606111512—$18.95

GODSPELLS: WRITTEN SPELLS, SPOKEN SPELLS AND SPELL ENHANCERS—Here are the rules laid down thousands of years ago by those who spoke with the Heavenly Host and learned of his TRUE wishes for all of mankind. NOT of the devil. For unselfish use only!
8.5x11—140 pages—ISBN-13: 978-0938294498—$18.95

COUNT SAINT GERMAIN - THE MAN WHO LIVES FOREVER — Let Count Saint Germain — the man who lives forever — help transform your life through his insight into the metaphysical laws that govern the universe. "Strange" bio by Art Crocket. Channelings of the Master by Wm Oribello.
8.5x11—132 pages—ISBN-13: 978-1892062208—$21.95
Add $20 for DVD of Oribello channeling Saint Germain under the purple ray.

CURSES AND THEIR REVERSALS— Plus: Omens, Superstitions And The Removal Of The Evil Eye. Important workbook by Oribello with Maria D' Andrea, Lady Suzanne and others.
8.5x11—182 pages—ISBN-13: 978-1606111406—$21.95

YOU CAN TAKE IT WITH YOU

www.ingramcontent.com/pod-product-compliance
Lightning Source LLC
Chambersburg PA
CBHW071119090426
42736CB00012B/1952